Velsmagende

Taihen Oishii

Very Tasty

Three Worlds

Cookbook

Velsmagende

Taihen Oishii

Very Tasty

Three Worlds Cookbook

GAYLE AND ROBERT
FLETCHER ALLEN

Keats Publishing, Inc.

NEW CANAAN, CONNECTICUT

VELSMAGENDE   TAIHEN OISHII   VERY TASTY
THREE WORLDS COOKBOOK

ISBN: 0-87983-096-4
Library of Congress Catalog Card Number: 75-19542

Printed in the United States of America

Keats Publishing, Inc.
36 Grove Street, New Canaan, Connecticut 06840, U.S.A.

For Liz, who patiently waited at home
while her parents were off
traipsing the face of the earth

Contents

viii

Foreword

We love to cook. We enjoy it for a number of reasons, some important to our family and friends, others important only to us. Cooking is one of the most creative and constructive activities we know.

If you follow these recipes step by step, ingredient by ingredient, you can be assured of success and good nutrition. But if, as you go along, you put a bit of your own imagination and invention into the process you will gain an even greater satisfaction. Granted, the recipes in this book may not be your own, but the interpretation and preparation can be. As you will note many of the recipes presented here are followed by variations. Some of these simply show an alternate way to prepare a dish or give alternate ingredients that may be used while others are sheer invention. Approach this book with the same spirit of invention and create your own variations as you go along. We have a close friend who is a good cook. She follows every recipe down to the tiniest detail. Someday when she finds herself temporarily out of a certain spice, condiment or seasoning and adds a small substitute touch of her own, she will be on the way to becoming a great cook.

Of equal importance in preparing meals for family and friends is to present the best quality and freshest foods available. Unfortunately, few people look up from a nutritiously planned and carefully prepared meal to comment on the variety of health-giving vitamins and minerals that are included. It is up to us, the cooks, to see that food is not only of the highest nutritional value but also presents a pleasing aspect to both the eye and the palate.

All of the recipes presented here can be easily adapted for nutritional benefit. Use fresh vegetables and fruits in season and buy those that are organically grown, if possible. If you must use canned foods, choose them carefully from a known source at your health food store. Use only meat and fish of the highest quality. When preparing foods use raw sugar, fructose, or honey when a recipe calls for sugar. Similarly substitute brown rice for rice, sea salt for salt, unbleached flour for flour, and always use an oil that is polyunsaturated or cold-pressed. Once the mind accepts the fact that natural foods are best for vibrant health, the body will respond and thank us for it.

The recipes in this book were carefully gathered during travels that have taken us over much of the surface of the earth. In our opinion they are the best of literally thousands of dishes we sampled. All of these recipes have been tested many times in our own kitchen in proportions that serve four to six people, unless otherwise specified. The recipes set in bold face may be located by consulting the index.

The Very Old World—

Japan

A lthough the precise origin of the Japanese people is obscure, it is generally agreed that they migrated from the arid wind-blown steppes of northern Asia, crossing the shallow Sea of Japan from what is now Siberia and Korea. With them they brought a lust for adventure and a unique culture, but more important, the desire for a better life. These early emigrants found themselves in a land of verdant mountains, grassy meadows, beautiful valleys, and above all, in proximity to vast areas of ocean waters, which were teeming with many varieties of fish and other aquatic life. These foods were to become the mainstay of their diet.

The first settlers felt a strong desire to live in harmony with nature and their worship of nature eventually evolved into the Shinto religion. Of the many Shinto deities that emerged, the food goddess Ukemochi-no-kami is one of the most important.

This close tie with nature has dominated every facet of Japanese life and has markedly influenced their eating habits. Nowhere is natural food more emphasized than in Japan, and the true secret of Japanese cooking lies in using the freshest ingredients to obtain a natural flavor. The quality of food served is uppermost in the minds of Japanese cooks whether they be housewives or restaurateurs. Housewives generally shop before every meal and use foods in season to assure the utmost quality and freshness of all meats and vegetables. The women of Japan have been concerned with the natural freshness of food for so long that it has become second nature to them. Many Japanese housewives are now demanding organically-grown vegetables and meats.

Further evidence of the Japanese demand for natural foods is the extensive consumption of fish. For many Japanese families the day begins with a fish soup for breakfast. So clever are the cooks, that although fish may be served every day, it is always *taihen oishii*—very tasty.

The use of oils and fats or vegetable shortening is almost nonexistent in most Japanese recipes. Strong, overpowering flavors are not characteristic of this cuisine. Instead most flavors are subtle, with light delicate tastes predominating. Even soy sauce, though pungent in flavor, is used sparingly so as not to overpower the more subtle tastes. The one exception to this is the saltiness produced by the Japanese habit of cooking with seaweed. This generous use of salt is traditional and is designed to make the diner thirsty so that he will consume and enjoy the beer or sake served with the meal. If you are concerned about the amount of salt in your diet (and everyone should be) you will be comforted to know that all the recipes in this book have been adjusted to American tastes, and it would be unwise to further reduce the amount of salt specified. In preparing these delicacies in our kitchen, we have attempted to strike a happy medium for both taste and good health. Use whole sea salt to get those valuable trace minerals.

There is something exquisitely simple about food as it is presented by the Japanese. They have a great regard and love for beauty so they will enhance the flavors of a dish by making it more pleasing to the eye. Whether for a small bite of raw fish or a complete meal, great attention is given to detail and attractive presentation. We really feel this is the greatest way not only to enjoy food, but also to eat for health's sake.

According to an old saying in Japan, "If one experiences a new taste in life, that life will be lengthened by many days." We sincerely hope that it is true, for if it is, all of the readers of this book will enjoy an enviable longevity.

Almost all the recipes given to us by friends in Japan have many variations, so when reading them, please don't feel that they must be followed precisely to the letter. Indeed, if you are a creative cook, you should find great pleasure in changing any and all to suit your own family's taste.

How about some soup?

Because of its versatility, nutrition, and taste appeal, soup in almost any form is certainly an international favorite. Some Japanese soups are complicated in preparation, others extremely simple. We want you to enjoy the *best* of these wonderful concoctions. Here they are.

Basic
Clear
Soup
SERVES 4

1 quart water
1 teaspoon or 1-inch section dried kelp
¼ cup bonita (dried or fresh)
¼ teaspoon lemon juice

Bring the water and kelp to a boil and simmer for 1 minute. Cover and let stand 1 minute. Remove the kelp. Add the lemon juice and bonita and cook slowly for about 3 minutes. Take off fire and strain for a lovely clear broth. Keep covered until serving time and then serve in individual covered bowls, keeping the flavor locked in at all times.

This soup may be served as is, or with a variety of garnishes to create distinctively different taste sensations. Thinly peel and twist a bit of lemon peel, add a tiny morsel of cooked chicken, or perhaps a piece of cooked whitefish.

While visiting in the home of a Japanese friend near Osaka we were served this unusual treat. The two daughters-in-law who prepared the meal gave us the recipe, and we were also privileged to tour the kitchen and see the method of preparation.

This is a steamed soup and if you are fortunate enough to have a Japanese steamer you are way ahead. They are available throughout the world, since Japanese cuisine is gaining international popularity. Lacking a steamer, you may use any large cooking pot with a snug-fitting lid.

In the bottom of a pot place any food can that is about 3 inches in diameter and 2 to 3 inches in height. On top of the can place a heat-proof plate or pie tin (we use the steamer ring from a pressure cooker). Fill the pot with water to within 1 inch of the bottom of the can. Now you have a steamer.

Custard Soup
SERVES 4

4 shrimp

½ chicken breast, boned

CUSTARD

3 large eggs

2½ cups chicken broth

½ teaspoon soy sauce

Cook the shrimp until tender and pink, then cool and split in half. Cook the chicken until tender, then cut in small squares. Place 2 shrimp halves and 2 or 3 pieces of chicken in the bottom of individual 6-ounce oven-proof custard cups.

Beat the eggs until fluffy. Add the chicken broth and soy sauce (Japanese housewives use **Basic clear soup** instead of the chicken broth). Pour the custard over the shrimp and chicken to within 1 inch of the top of the cup. Skim off the bubbles. The cups are placed in the steamer on the pie plate and the steamer is covered tightly. Bring the water to a boil, turn the heat to medium, and steam for about 10 minutes, or until slightly firm.

Seafood and Melon Soup
SERVES 4

4 to 8 medium shrimp

2 cups clear chicken stock or broth

1 tablespoon soy sauce

1 tablespoon sweet sake or sherry

1 lemon leaf or 1-inch piece lemon rind (optional)

4 to 8 1-inch cubes fresh honeydew melon

Cook the shrimp in boiling water until pink and tender, about 5 minutes. Immediately plunge into cold water. Shell, devein and set aside. Add the soy sauce and sake or sherry to the stock. If you have access to a lemon leaf, add one now (a 1-inch strip of fresh lemon rind may be substituted) and slowly simmer the broth for about 5 minutes. Remove the lemon before adding the melon. With the broth just barely simmering, add the pieces of melon and cook until just tender, using a sharp fork to test for degree of doneness. When the tip of the tine slips easily into the melon, remove the melon pieces from the broth. Arrange 1 or 2 shrimp and 1 or 2 melon cubes in each bowl. Add steaming broth to the bowl and serve immediately.

Many soups are so nourishing and satisfying that an entire meal may be made in one pot. This soup is garnished with shitake *(large Japanese dried mushrooms) and egg curls, both of which are prepared in advance of the broth.*

To prepare the shitake, *soak in enough water to completely cover and float them. They will swell up and become soft. If you cannot find* shitake, *use very large brown mushrooms. Slice the mushrooms and instead of soaking, cook them in water to cover until soft and tender.*

Vegetable, Fish and Egg Garnish Soup

EGG CURLS
2 eggs
¼ teaspoon sea salt
   polyunsaturated oil

BROTH
1 quart water
1 vegetable cube
1 teaspoon dried kelp or dried bonita
¼ cup white fish
1 small carrot, grated
¼ pound fresh spinach
¼ teaspoon raw sugar
1 teaspoon soy sauce

In a large bowl beat the eggs until they are well blended and light in color, using a wire whisk or blender. Add the salt. For cooking the curls use a cast-iron skillet, 6 inches in diameter (this produces a near-perfect size). Heat the skillet and brush with the cooking oil. Pour in just enough egg to coat the bottom of the skillet, rolling the skillet slightly to level the egg. As soon as it is firm, tip the skillet and push one edge toward the center, using chopsticks or a small spatula. Remove the egg pancakes from the skillet to an absorbent paper towel. Roll each pancake tightly and set aside to cool. Continue cooking the egg mixture until all is used. When it is time to serve the soup, cut these egg rolls into ½-inch slices.

To make broth, bring the water to a boil and boil the vegetable cube until completely dissolved. Add the kelp or bonita and simmer about 2 minutes, then remove kelp or strain to remove bonita. While slowly simmering, add bits of fish, grated carrot and spinach. While this is simmering add the raw sugar and soy sauce. Simmer for several minutes.

Arrange the egg curls and mushrooms in the bottom of individual soup bowls and very slowly pour in a small amount of the soup. Let the mushrooms and egg curls settle to the bottom, then pour full of soup. Pouring this way will allow the mushrooms and egg curls to stay on the bottom of the bowl rather than float to the top.

Another word about soups

Almost all one-pot cookery ends by serving the broth at the end of the meal, so we would venture to say that there is hardly a Japanese meal without soup in some form or other. We often reflect that the broth, pot liquor or juices which many cooks throw away, may not only be the most delectable in flavor but also have excellent nutrition for our bodies. Next time you have eaten the last of the green beans or other vegetables, save the pot liquor and start a soup.

This soup is dominated by a distinctive soybean flavor, and it may take more than one serving to acquire the taste for it, for it has a "oneness" flavor. This is a good transitional dish between courses, a way to clear the palate from one taste to another.

Tofu *is a bean curd. It is made from soybeans, providing the diet with nourishing proteins* Tofu *usually is found in small 3-inch squares. It is served as is, or cut into thirds for subtler use in soups and certain main dishes.* Tofu *may be purchased in most Japanese markets in fresh cakes or in powdered form.*

Tofu Custard Soup

tofu cake

CUSTARD
3 cups water
½ teaspoon dried kelp
1 tablespoon dried bonita
¼ teaspoon soy sauce
4 eggs
freshly grated ginger root

To make this custard-on-custard soup, begin by placing a 1½ inch square of *Tofu* cake into the bottom of individual custard cups.

Simmer water, kelp, bonita and soy sauce for about ten minutes. Strain and cool. Beat the eggs until light in color, then fold into the cooled liquid. Pour this over the *tofu* in the custard cups, about two-thirds full. Cover tightly and steam for about 12 minutes, or until firm. See instructions for steaming on page 15.

Serve with freshly grated ginger root and let each person use this garnish to individual taste.

Sometimes a sweet soup is served toward the end of the meal.

Sweet Soybean Soup

1 quart water

1- inch strip dried kelp

¼ cup dried or fresh bonita

2 or 3 tablespoons red or white table wine

soybean paste

1 young green onion or white turnip

Boil the water and add kelp. Simmer for about 1 minute and remove kelp, otherwise the soup will be too salty. Add the bonita and remove from the fire. Cover and let stand for several minutes to absorb the flavor. Strain through a cheesecloth, leaving a beautifully clear soup stock. Add the wine and a small amount of soybean paste, starting with several tablespoons and adding to your taste. Stir with a wire whisk. Continue to simmer until thoroughly heated. As a garnish for this soup, use a bit of finely shredded green onion or white turnip.

It is easy to see that most Japanese soups appear to be very much the same. It's amazing how distinct the flavors and taste sensations actually are after sampling.

Quick Clear Soup

2 10¾-ounce cans chicken broth

1 tablespoon soy sauce

1 tablespoon sweet sake or sherry

½ teaspoon freshly ground ginger

Combine all the ingredients, bring to a boil, and simmer for several minutes. Serve in covered bowls to keep the steaming flavor intact.

Variations   Add fresh lemon rind as a garnish to produce a subtle lemony flavor.

Add fresh watercress, a small sprig of parsley, or a bit of shredded carrot. Any vegetable in season will change the flavor of this soup in a distinctive way.

On the following pages there are dozens of exciting main dishes and specialties to tantalize your family and guests, so you might wish to "cheat" a little with soup preparation. Carefully shop for a variety of prepackaged Japanese soups in health food stores or Japanese markets.

Sashimi—a different form of fish

Probably the best example of Japanese insistence on quality is seen in the preparation of *sashimi*—raw fish, expertly sliced and served in individually prepared portions. It is served either plain or with a mild soy sauce. The most widely used fish for *sashimi* is tuna, but a genuine fan may enjoy as many as a dozen varieties of fresh, uncooked fish at one sitting. As for quality, when you are served *sashimi* it is the best, and if it were not, you would not be served at all. When last visiting Kyoto we were taken to a very fine restaurant. Because of our rigorous schedule the dinner hour was quite late. When we arrived we found the place closed up tight. The reason? Not the late dining hour. The owner of the restaurant had run out of his top quality fish and had simply closed the restaurant rather than serve an inferior meal.

When we serve *sashimi* we try to buy the fish at a market that specializes in *fresh* fish. Usually if they have fish suitable for *sashimi*, it will be displayed and labeled as such. If you patronize a Japanese market, they are usually glad to slice the fish for you. Perhaps if time allows, they will instruct you in proper slicing techniques. Some may even share a favorite dipping sauce with you.

We understand that raw fish is good for the digestion. However, if serving at home or eating in restaurants unknown to you, be careful. We are advised by a physician friend that there can be harmful parasites in certain raw fish, so top quality is all-important.

Of the following varieties, choose the freshest and the finest quality you can obtain.

tuna	sea bass
abalone	bream
red snapper	squid
bass	eel

Using any one or several of the above, filet, remove all the bones, and slice *paper thin*. It is properly sliced when individual slices may be held up to the kitchen light and you are able to distinguish the vague image of the light fixture itself through the slice.

Presentation Inasmuch as this is often the main course, the presentation deserves special attention. Since the fish is white or nearly transparent, colorful surroundings to the dish are important. Select an elaborately-designed platter and arrange the *sashimi* slices in a distinctive symmetrical pattern.

Now for some colorful garnish. Freshly picked parsley or mint with a crisp green look is particularly effective. Also, a number of thinly pared carrot swirls with small bits of tomato or red pepper give a subtle color accent.

When fish and garnish have been arranged, cover with plastic wrap and refrigerate. (Do not refrigerate for more than 1 hour.)

The Japanese white radish is shaped like a carrot but is a bit larger and fatter overall and quite white. We were driving along a busy street in Osaka one morning when our car passed a truckload of these white radishes going to market. When we commented on them, our interpreter told us that in Japan the white radish is known affectionately as "lady's legs," because they are quite smooth, white, and shaped somewhat like a woman's leg.

Dipping Sauce

½ cup soy sauce

1 tablespoon lemon or lime juice

a dash white pepper

1 tablespoon grated white turnip (this is reasonably close to the Japanese white radish in taste and appearance)

1 tablespoon warm sake (optional)

Combine all the ingredients and simmer for about 5 minutes. Pour into small individual dipping cups and serve. This is a delicious, mild sauce.

Green horseradish is called wasahi. *It may be purchased in powdered form. It is quite strong and we think it best to let each person add it to the sauce as his taste dictates. Better too little than too much. Also, you can work up to a stronger sauce as you progress with the* sashimi.

A Stronger Sauce

¼ cup sake

½ cup soy sauce

1 tablespoon green horseradish

Combine the sake and soy sauce and simmer. Mix the *wasahi* with enough cold water to make a paste. Cover and let stand for about 20 minutes. When the sauce is heated and poured into dipping bowls, place a dab of *wasahi* beside it on the serving plate.

A very special abalone

Several summers ago our son worked on Catalina Island off the coast of California. While there he caught several good abalone. One day he brought home an abalone "fresh from the sea" and instead of pounding the fish (the usual preparation technique) and frying, we sliced it thin for *sashimi*. We were all treated to a delicate new taste experience.

By introducing new tastes to children as they are growing up, you set the stage for eating enjoyment and, as important, good nutrition, as they grow older. We believe that if you tease the taste buds and introduce as many good, nutritious foods as possible to the offspring, they will always be led to appreciate new foods. Treat the dining experience as a total atmosphere rather than a quick satisfaction of hunger. Everyone profits from the experience.

A final thought on *sashimi*

Begin with perhaps tuna alone for this delicacy. It doesn't really taste like fish per se, but rather like rare roast beef with a subtle hint of tuna in the background. As you find your taste tantalized, proceed with other varieties of fish.

Here's a way for you to try raw fish for the first time without going all the way. Rice sushi is really a little rice sandwich with a vinegary flavor and just a tiny bit of raw fish in the center.

Sushi may be prepared at the very minute of consumption or hours ahead. They may be extremely simple or very elaborate, plain or wrapped in sheets of nori, a type of seaweed purchased in very thin sheets. Nori is charcoal in color with a hint of green. When you warm the sheets to wrap around the rice cakes, they change color to a deep purplish-black. You can buy the nori in Japanese markets and it keeps well for months. If you cannot find the nori in shops near you, make the sushi plain. They are delicious with or without the fish, or with vegetable substitutes.

Rice
Sushi

2 cups brown rice

1-inch square kelp (if available)

4 tablespoons white vinegar or 3 tablespoons white vinegar and 1 tablespoon mirin (sweet sake used in cooking) or sherry

1 teaspoon sea salt

3 tablespoons raw sugar

Wash the rice in cool water and drain. Do this about three times.

Into a 2-quart heat-proof dish (pyrex or ceramic) pour 3 cups cold water. Add the kelp, if available, and the rice. Cover and let stand for 20 minutes. Put into a preheated 350°F. oven for 1 hour, or until all the water has been absorbed. Remove from the oven and quickly add the mixture of vinegar, salt and sugar. Mix thoroughly and cover tightly. This is a little like steeping a pot of tea. When completely cooled it is ready to form the *sushi*. You can make this ahead of time as it keeps for hours.

Wrapped sushi   If you are going to roll your *sushi* in seaweed, place a warmed sheet of *nori* on a coarse cloth (any cotton or linen material will work well—the Japanese usually use a bamboo placemat). Fill the seaweed down the center with the rice mixture and pat evenly to the edges until covered to within about 1 inch of the edge. Make a little trough in the center and fill with a thin sliver of fish.

Roll gently over and over into as tight a roll as possible. Let rest for about 10 minutes to set the shape then carefully remove the cloth. Put into the refrigerator to quicken the setting process. When thoroughly cooled, use a sharp knife to cut cross-rounds about 1 inch wide. You have rice *sushi*.

These little morsels keep very well. Put them in picnic baskets, school lunches or serve with your Japanese meal.

Easy unwrapped method   Lightly wipe a cookie sheet with a bit of oil to prevent sticking. Pat the rice mixture out until about ¾ inch thick. With a very sharp knife score the top lengthwise and crosswise into 1½-inch squares. Place a tiny morsel of raw fish on each square and gently press in with your finger. Cover and cool until serving time, then cut on scored lines and slide off with a spatula. Arrange on a tray like finger sandwiches, or serve several on individual dishes. A slim lemon peel is a handsome garnish.

Variations   If you prefer not to use the raw fish, substitute any cooked fish, pungent pickle, meat, or vegetable. The more colorful, the better.

Another variation is to roll the rice *sushi* mixture into a ball (about the size of a golf ball) and press bits of colorful garnish into the sides. Serve as an accompaniment to cooked fish. *Sushi* will complement any main course.

If you like sesame seeds, roll the *sushi* in them, adding a simple colorful garnish as well. Cracked sunflower or pumpkin seeds are equally as good. Roasting the seeds helps too.

Sushi Hors d'Oeuvre

Marinate thin slices of halibut in lemon juice for about 3 hours. Put a ½-inch ball of rice *sushi* on a thin strip of the marinated fish and roll into a ball. These can be served plain or with a garnish.

If serving as a finger food, place a damp cloth on the plate as they are a bit sticky. Speaking of a damp cloth . . .

Oshibori: a most pleasing and refreshing custom

The *oshibori* is a cloth, much like a regular washcloth, that has been dampened, rung out, and rolled up like a jellyroll. In winter these are placed on a rack and kept hot with steam. In summer they are kept chilled.

These are presented before the meal and the diner wipes the face and hands. The *oshibori* is not only designed for cleanliness, but also for refreshment.

Rice

Europeans have their breads, Italians have their pasta, and the Japanese have rice. This staple is eaten three times a day by most Japanese. Their rice is not fluffy but rather heavy and sticky, thus easier to eat with chopsticks. In Japan rice is served in an individual dish, perhaps an equivalent to the Westerner's bread and butter plate.

Wash the grains of rice several times. Cover with cold water and let stand for 1 hour before cooking. Cook either the conventional way in boiling water on top of the stove, or in the oven as described in the preparation of *sushi*.

If cooking on top of the stove, a good rule to follow is to use 1½ cups of water for each cup of rice to be cooked. It is best to start the rice in cold water and bring to the boil rather than add the rice to already boiling water. Cook the rice for 20 minutes then drain and let stand another 5 minutes to set.

If you have rice left over and wish to reheat it, place in a sieve or colander over boiling water, cover, and steam for about 10 minutes. If you don't have a pot with a lid, use aluminum foil to make a cover. Steaming will maintain the consistency of the rice, whereas oven reheating tends to dry it out.

In Japan, a cleaned rice bowl signifies that you are quite content and fully satisfied with the meal and want for nothing else. A bit left in the bowl is a signal that you would like more. Friends in Japan explained that rice is served at the end of the meal to insure that the guest has had enough to eat.

A final thought on rice: We would not suggest you buy Japanese rice, as they remove the outer layer before consumption, thus removing the vital B-complex vitamin, losing much of the nutritional value. This is done to remove residual traces of radioactivity, still persisting after the atomic holocaust over Nagasaki and Hiroshima in 1945. Instead, buy brown rice and cook by the same method.

Main Dishes

The flavor of prepared foods in Japan begins with the raw materials. The development of prime, top quality meats, for example, starts "on the hoof," where extraordinary care is taken to produce a beef of excellence.

Matsuzaka beef is perhaps the finest in taste and texture we will ever experience. The farmers who produce this beef are truly artists. Rarely do these experts raise more than three steers simultaneously. Beginning usually with one steer and adding one each year for the ensuing two years, the farmer then has one steer ready for market every year, acquiring a new calf to replace the steer ready for consumption.

The steers live a life of distinct isolation, often in air-conditioned stalls, where they are hand-massaged to evenly distribute a unique marbleizing of fat. The feedstuffs are carefully selected grains and hay of an ultimate quality. They are also fed beer for the digestion and weight gain. The steers are pampered and attended with such loving care, it is no wonder that the meat is so tender and delicious.

Because this beef is produced for such ultimate quality, freezing is considered out of the question. Once having had Matsuzaka beef, the diner will be hard-pressed to ever find anything to compare.

Close to Matsuzaka beef

Start with the finest grade of well marbled filet, top sirloin or rib steak available. Chill the beef in the freezer until it is very cold. Sharpen your finest slicing knife and carefully cut into slices no more than ¼ inch thick. Have the serving plates warm. Heat a cast-iron skillet until very hot, then brush with vegetable oil. When a bead of water sizzles and disappears, the pan is ready. Sear the slices for 1 minute on each side and arrange on the serving plates or a platter. Put 1 tablespoon soy sauce into the hot skillet and roll it around from side to side, letting the soy mix with the meat juices. Do not put back on the fire. Spoon a little of the sauce on each slice of beef.

Teriyaki

Teriyaki is another favorite around our house, served in the form of steaks, hamburgers, kabobs and as hors d'oeuvres. Let's get started by preparing the basic **Teriyaki sauce.**

This sauce is the basis for all teriyaki *dishes.*

Teriyaki Sauce

1 tablespoon white vinegar, lemon juice, sake or papaya juice (this will provide natural tenderizing for the meat)

½ cup cream sherry

½ cup soy sauce

½ teaspoon ground ginger (freshly grated root if possible)

1 clove garlic, minced or crushed

½ teaspoon finely ground pepper

Steak Teriyaki

Use any cut of meat suitable for serving as a steak, including rib and other cuts. The **Teriyaki sauce** just given is enough for 4 to 6 steaks weighing between ½ and ¾ pounds each.

Place the sauce in a flat dish and dip steaks, coating both sides. Pat the sauce into the meat and let stand at room temperature. Repeat the dipping process in 20 minutes. Let stand at room temperature for another 20 minutes. Cook on an outdoor grill or barbecue, or cook in the broiler, 2 inches from the flame, for about 5 minutes on each side for a 1-inch thick steak, medium rare. Decrease cooking time 1 minute for each ¼ inch less thickness.

To pan fry, have the skillet hot, brush with vegetable oil and sear, over medium heat, 5 minutes on each side, for a medium steak. Add the remaining sauce to the still-hot skillet, along with 1 tablespoon sake for each ½ cup sauce. Serve separately for guests to dip individual bites of steak during the meal.

Teriyaki Hamburgers
SERVES 4

If American-style hamburgers can be served on the Ginza in Tokyo, we can certainly serve *teriyaki*-style hamburgers anywhere in the world.

For 4 hamburger patties to be eaten as is, or in a bun, you will need 1 full pound lean ground beef. Do buy the lean—and organically produced, if available—rather than regular hamburger.

Put the lean beef into a medium-sized bowl and break into pieces with your hands. Knead at least ½ cup of the **Teriyaki sauce** (more if you can) into the meat. Form patties and let rest for 20 minutes. Cook as you normally would, adding a dash of sea salt to the hot skillet to prevent sticking as the lean beef will produce little fat.

Save the drippings in the skillet and while the pan is still hot, put back on low heat and add 2 tablespoons very hot water, stirring quickly with a wooden spoon or spatula. Serve the hamburgers plain topped with some of the liquid, or serve on buns, dipping the buns into the hot juice.

Teriyaki Kabobs

You will need approximately ⅓ pound of beef (preferably top sirloin or sirloin tip) for each person to be served. If available in your area, use braising strips. These are the "tails" cut from the porterhouse steak.

With a very sharp knife slice the beef into 1-inch wide strips, then cut cross-grain into still smaller pieces about ¼-inch thick. You may eventually prefer 1-inch cubes, but for the time being, let's do it as the Japanese do.

Put the strips of beef into a full recipe of the **Teriyaki sauce**, cover, and refrigerate overnight. Keep tightly sealed or everything in the refrigerator will absorb the pungent taste of the sauce. Using thin bamboo skewers, which are available in most markets, twist 4 to 6 pieces of the marinated steak onto each. Prepare all and let rest at room temperature until ready to cook. Broil in a preheated oven, about 2 inches from the heat source for about 3 minutes on each side for medium rare.

Teriyaki kabobs are also perfect for outdoor cooking. If you are serving a large group, put the beef on the skewers well in advance of marinating.

As for the sauce recipe, we use it as written for our family, doubled for company and quadrupled for a large outdoor gathering.

Variation Our favorite use of *teriyaki* kabobs is with chunks of fresh pineapple and strawberries and lemonade served alongside.

These are decidedly at their best when fresh-made but may be frozen with good results. They are mighty handy for unexpected guests.

Teriyaki Hors d'Oeuvre

1 recipe Teriyaki sauce
1 pound top sirloin, flank or filet steak
baking parchment paper

Slice the sirloin cross-grain into thin bite-size pieces. Cutting cross-grain makes the meat infinitely more tender. Put pieces in a pot with the sauce and marinate for several hours or overnight.

Cut parchment paper into 4-inch squares. Place one bite of meat into the center of each paper square and spoon ½ teaspoon of the **Teriyaki sauce** on top. Bring the two sides of the parchment together up and over the meat. When the two sides are touching, fold together and down ¼ inch, then over itself another ¼ inch. You now have a double fold. Pat down until somewhat flattened, then crimp the two ends upward and flatten. Refrigerate or freeze until ready to cook.

Preheat the oven to 400°F. Place as many of the packages as possible on a cookie sheet and bake for 10 minutes. If frozen, allow more time as the meat must thaw, then cook (about 15 to 20 minutes).

Variation Place unwrapped meat and sauce in a tightly-covered dish and bake as above, then remove cover for an additional 5 minutes cooking. Serve on toothpicks.

Be sure to serve your guests an *oshibori* that has been dipped into lemon water. A little lemon in the warm water will help to remove not only the stickiness, but the odor as well.

Chicken Teriyaki

Allow at least one-half chicken breast per person. Debone the chicken breast or have the butcher do it, then have him put it through the meat tenderizer or pound it flat. Soak in **Teriyaki sauce** for several hours, then either broil, grill or pan fry.

We cook the chicken differently than steak. Sear the chicken on both sides quickly, turn down the fire, and continue cooking. Add 2 tablespoons boiling water to the pan juices and serve ladled over the chicken.

If you grill indoors or outside, add 1 tablespoon sake to ½ cup sauce and heat for dipping. An extra bit of ground ginger enhances the sauce.

Barbecued Shrimp

Buy 3 or 4 large shrimp per person. The number will depend on what else you are serving with the shrimp.

Shell and devein the shrimp. Twist on skewers and cook. (They twist on better if you put a knife through where the vein was removed, leaving the shrimp cut almost in half and semi-butterflied.) Place in a shallow pan or lightly buttered cookie sheet. Pour the **Teriyaki sauce** over the shrimp and sprinkle uniformly with the juice of ½ lemon. Cover and let stand for several hours in the refrigerator. Remove 20 minutes before cooking to bring to room temperature. Broil or barbecue on a grill for about 2 minutes each side. Serve the remaining sauce to which a little more lemon juice and a dash of ginger has been added. Hot mustard is also excellent as a flavor accent.

Teppanyaki *is an especially popular dish in modern-day Japan and Korea. It can be cooked right at the table using a large electric skillet. You may also use an ordinary skillet set on a hot plate.*

In Japan there are a number of restaurants that specialize in this dish. It is so dramatically prepared that the accomplished dexterity of the chef, his hands flying, becomes as graceful as a skilled circus juggler.

In Japan, this dish is prepared for as few as two, or as many as ten or twelve diners, and at the table. There is usually a griddle built into the table, level with the dining surface. The meat is normally brought out for the diners' inspection as it is being weighed. The chef then cuts the beef into thin strips just exactly the right size for single bites. This is done so swiftly, we have always feared for the fingers!

A tray is arranged with these tender morsels and another with mushrooms, onions, and bean sprouts. Sometimes, for a really elaborate meal, both beef and shrimp are served. Fresh garlic is chopped and spread through the oil on the griddle, with the hands of the cook flying high in the air, crossing, over and out to swish the garlic with true artistry. Each food is cooked in front of you and pushed toward each diner as it is ready.

This recipe, although authentic, certainly cannot possibly contain all of the flourish witnessed in Japan; however the same taste is there.

Teppanyaki

⅓ pound top sirloin or filet of beef per person

2 to 3 small shrimp per person (optional)

¼ sliced brown onion per person

¼ pound large mushrooms, sliced

¼ pound bean sprouts per person

¼ cup rice, prepared Japanese-style, per person

several cloves of garlic, depending on personal taste. Authentic teppanyaki requires considerable garlic, however the preparation seems to tone down its strength.

sea salt and pepper to taste

2 tablespoons vegetable oil

About 1 hour before serving, slice the beef cross-grain into bite-sized strips. Slice the garlic into a flat dish. Add salt and pepper to taste. Roll the meat in this mixture and knead until thoroughly blended. Cover and set aside. Arrange the onions and mushrooms in slices beside a mound of bean sprouts.

Preheat an electric skillet to 375°F. When ready to cook, rub a 1-inch square of beef fat over the surface of the skillet and discard the fat. Add the chopped garlic and 1 tablespoon vegetable oil. Cook quickly until the garlic has a toasted appearance then remove. Put several beef pieces into the skillet and quickly sear. Push the cooked bites toward your guests or have them serve themselves with chopsticks. Inasmuch as the cooking can be half the fun, encourage the guests to cook their own.

If you are also serving shrimp, cook the same way, but as an individual course, not at the same time as the beef. Keep the taste sensations separated; it's the Japanese way.

The rice should be in small bowls or cups on the individual serving plates.

As soon as the meat is eaten, cook the onions and mushrooms. The last to be served will be the bean sprouts. Add the chopped cooked garlic to the remaining 1 tablespoon vegetable oil and the bean sprouts. Move them around the skillet until limp, then let rest. Stir from time to time.

A special addition   Mix equal parts crunchy peanut butter and sweet hot mustard together. Put about 1 tablespoonful in a small cup or dish beside each guest.

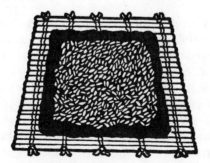

This dish is famous all over the world as one of the most authentic Japanese dishes. However, it was created for the visiting tourist, since the Japanese, in their effort to please Westerners, think that this may be the taste that comes closest to the Western diet. We have enjoyed sukiyaki *many times and in many places, but it was never better than in Japan.*

Our Japanese friend in Osaka gave us this recipe after we had enjoyed it in her home. Her very literal English began with: "For five man." The recipe is for five, rather than our traditional four, for in Japan, the number four means bad luck.

Sukiyaki
(pronounced skee-yaki)

⅓ pound lean beef (filet or top sirloin) per person, sliced into very thin slices

shirataki (long near-transparent noodles, may be bought in cans)

bamboo shoots

water chestnuts

shitake or large brown mushrooms

green onions

Chinese cabbage

watercress

spinach

bean sprouts

tofu cakes

zucchini

1   cup soy sauce

1   cup sweet sake (mirin)

½   cup raw sugar

All of these items should be of peak quality. Wash, then cut or slice as attractively as possible and neatly arrange on a large tray or platter.

Preheat an electric skillet or heavy cast-iron one on a hot plate to 400°F. Rub with a 1-inch square of beef fat and discard.

Have ready a container with the soy sauce, another with the sake and a small dish of raw sugar with a tablespoon measure in it.

Put some of the meat slices into the skillet, sear quickly, turn and pour about ¼ cup soy sauce overy the meat. Sprinkle with 2 tablespoons sugar, Add about one-third of the vegetables, in separate piles, in order of their cooking time. Pour about ¼ cup sake over all. The liquid should bubble as the items in the skillet are moved about for cooking. When everything is done, each person takes portions from the skillet as he chooses.

Use extra soy sauce, sake and sugar when you add fresh ingredients to the skillet during the meal. *Sukiyaki* is served with warm sake and Japanese beer.

When *sukiyaki* is served in Japan, each diner is given a small dish beside his plate containing a whole egg in the shell. Prior to taking the *sukiyaki* from the pan, the diner breaks the raw egg into the dish and whips it until frothy with chopsticks. Each bite is then dipped into the egg and eaten.

This tempting dish, consisting of bits of fish and vegetables dipped in batter and deep-fried, was borrowed from Portuguese traders centuries ago. It is nevertheless associated with the Japanese cuisine in a special way.

The average serving should be 2 or 3 of each item prepared. Shrimp (or any fish you enjoy in small portions), mushrooms, green beans, brown onion, sweet potato and carrots are all very suitable to this nutritious dish.

Tempura

shrimp
sweet potatoes
selection of vegetables

BATTER
¾ cup unbleached flour
1 tablespoon arrowroot
pinch sea salt
1 cup very cold water
1 egg

For the *tempura*, first clean and devein the shrimp. Leave the tails attached to serve as a handle later. With a sharp knife, cut through the center of the back, leaving the two halves together in butterfly fashion.

Pare and cut the sweet potatoes into ¼-inch slices. Wash and cut the other vegetables into bite-sized pieces. Arrange on a large platter.

Sift the dry ingredients. Using a wire whisk, stir in the cold water. Slightly beat the egg and add, stirring constantly. The batter should be thin enough to run easily off a spoon. If it appears too thick, add a little more cold water.

In a heavy deep fryer heat polyunsaturated oil to 400°F. (If you enjoy the subtle flavor of sesame seed oil, use that.) Dip each piece of food in the tempura batter, swirl it around and let it drip. Fry in the hot oil until crispy. Remove the fried foods onto paper towels to absorb excess oil. You will be able to cook only a few pieces at a time. Keep warm on serving plates in the oven until ready to serve. The Japanese serve *tempura* with a sauce, as well as a small dish of salt and lemon wedges.

Dipping Sauce for Tempura

1 cup water
¼ cup soy sauce
1 tablespoon sweet sake or cream sherry
   freshly grated ginger

Warm in a small pan on the stove and add the freshly grated ginger just before serving.

Milder Tempura Sauce

½ cup soy sauce
½ cup chicken broth

Combine and warm.

The *tempura* is dipped in the sauce and accompanied by sake or beer.

We once asked a Japanese friend how she was able to prepare her *tempura* with such a fluffy appearance. She confided that while a portion of the food was frying, she dipped her fingers lightly into the batter and flung bits of extra batter toward the frying *tempura*. These extra bits of batter cling to the partially-cooked batter and indeed give an appearance of greater crispness.

This recipe for *tempura* brings back the memory of our first experience with the popularity of the Japanese sweet potato. On a cold rainy day while driving back to Osaka from Nara, the ancient capital city of centuries past, our car was passed by a small truck. As it passed us, a swirling cloud of greyish smoke rolled up from the back of the vehicle. We could clearly see a large metal box with a smoke-stack. We asked our driver if the truck driver was simply polluting the atmosphere or running the truck on wood. He laughed and then explained that the other driver was cooking sweet potatoes for his dinner, while returning from a pilgrimage to the great temple at Nara. The Japanese sweet potato is very popular as this little scene demonstrates.

Okonomi

This popular *tempura* dish is a deep-fried hors d'oeuvre. Any bite-sized food that appeals is dipped in batter and fried. Properly planned it can become a simple meal in itself, with guests seated informally around the table. Just keep dipping and cooking.

A Japanese friend who manufactures cooking utensils gave us a *tempura* cooker. There is an extra piece that fits over the bottom of the pan to prevent splattering. There is also a top grid on which to lay the cooked pieces to shed excess oils. These cookers are available today in many department stores. Although this cooker is definitely not a must by any means, it is a pleasure to use, even for dishes other than *tempura*.

Nabe is a do-it-yourself, all-in-one-pot, at-the-table, easy cooking technique. There are dozens of combinations, all delicious and nutritious. Use your imagination. When in Japan (and henceforth in your home) the rules of one-pot cooking are observed. There is one set of chopsticks for use in the pot, and one set to use in eating. The diner never uses his own for cooking. Also, the soup is drunk from the bowl, rather than spooned.

Nabe

(pronounced na-bee)

One-pot Cookery

chicken
beef
fish
vegetables

Use *any* or *all* of the ingredients. Cut them into small pieces.

Have an electric casserole dish or fondue pot on the table. Fill to within several inches of the top with chicken stock for chicken; fish broth for seafood; beef stock for beef. Have the vegetables of your choice arranged attractively on a platter. Using chopsticks (or fondue forks), swish each bite of food through the broth until cooked. The broth should be at least 325°F. throughout the meal. It is appropriate to use any accompanying sauce in this section, or any condiment you enjoy such as ginger, radish, turnip or mustard. After all the foods have been cooked, serve the broth in cups to be drunk as soup.

Yosenabe
(pronounced yo-sen-na-bee)

This literally means a little of everything . . . all in one pot. This dish differs from nabe *in that everything goes into the pot at the same time.*

One famous version of this dish takes place when Sumo wrestlers keep throwing items into the bubbling pot as it simmers for hours on end. They alternately wrestle and eat.

This is the Japanese equivalent of bouillabaisse. It can be brought to the table to serve, but we prefer to cook it at the table.

Prepare several seafoods of your choice by washing and cleaning. Lobster, clams, shrimp, crab and halibut are very good. These should be as fresh as possible. Use several vegetables, in season, such as Chinese cabbage, carrots, onions and watercress (all vitamin-packed) or any other favorite.

Also use *tofu* and *shirataki*. Cut the *tofu* into 1-inch squares and place in the bottom of each serving cup. The *shirataki* should be added to the broth a minute or two before serving time.

Use the **Basic clear soup** as the cooking liquid and have it bubbling. Guests may cook their own, but better here to put everything in the pot, except the *tofu* and noodles. Use chopsticks or fondue forks for swishing and eating. Finish by drinking the broth in cups.

The flavor of this dish is not strong, so a rather pungent dipping sauce is complementary.

Dipping Sauce for Yosenabe	½ cup soy sauce juice of 1 fresh lime (an old lime ferments slightly and loses its delicate flavor)

Combine ingredients.

Tips for using chopsticks

Many Japanese dishes simply would not taste the same eaten with a fork. After you have used wooden chopsticks, you will find something missing when you go back to using traditional utensils.

Hold one chopstick between the middle finger and the ring finger, at the first joint above the nail. Let it rest between the thumb and index finger, in the hollow next to the hand. This one will remain stationary.

Hold the second chopstick like a pencil, grasping between the thumb, at the nail, and the first joint of the index finger. Hold this one freely, moving it to meet the stationary chopstick. The tips of the chopsticks should extend two or three inches beyond where you are grasping them. The stationary chopstick goes on one side of the food and the other is moved so that it "pinches" the food between the two.

We Westerners, even if we have mastered the technique of eating with chopsticks, occasionally make the mistake of putting the tips of the chopstick into our mouths (similar to the use of a fork). This is incorrect. The Japanese hold the chopsticks up to their mouth with the sides parallel to the lips, taking the food from the side.

Desserts

Chances are that if you were to ask for dessert at the end of the meal in a restaurant in Japan, except one perhaps catering to a constant flow of tourists from the Western world, you would not be understood by the waiter. There is literally no such thing as dessert in Japan. The Japanese do enjoy sweet things, of course, but to destroy the delicate aftertaste of a fine meal with an American-type dessert is unthinkable.

Rather than dessert, let us think of this category of foods as the last course of the meal, that will both tantalize our thinking as well as tasting senses. Use lotus bowls in various colors or shapes, or if you have some particularly handsome oriental bowls, use them.

If you have an automatic rice warmer, use it now. In Japan these containers are usually akin to a giant thermos. They may be purchased anywhere in the world, as Japanese foods have become more popular. If you do not have such a utensil, keep the rice warm and steaming.

Have Japanese tea steaming in a teapot. We are supplied regularly with organically-grown green tea by friends in Japan, who fully understand our appreciation of that fine product. Many Japanese markets have similar tea available. It is a somewhat acquired taste. Or if you are not a fan of Japanese tea, perhaps your favorite herb tea. The light, aromatic varieties found in health food stores are very suitable on this occasion.

A variety of very sharp, pungent pickles are in order for this course of our meal. Ginger will complement also. Use any very tangy pickles or perhaps something you have created in a vinegary marinade. Melon rind is excellent.

Each person receives a bowl and a small plate of at least three varieties of pickle. The hostess serves each a healthy scoop of steaming rice. Pour tea over the rice to about two-thirds of the bowl. Each guest uses as much or as little of the pickle as he chooses. Most like to add a bit with each spoonful of rice and tea. This is about the only occasion for using a spoon. Not even the expert Japanese can handle tea with chopsticks.

The last course is most pleasing and satisfying, so I urge you to try it. It tends to calm the stomach and make one feel as though the digestive processes are working quietly and in perfect order. It also leaves you with a remembrance of the distinct flavors of the meal.

As with most foods of the Japanese cuisine, the last course is subtle. It is usually quite simple. It may, however, be served with a bit of added flourish, somehow signaling that it is the last, and therefore deserving of a little extra attention to end the occasion on best terms with the guests.

Perhaps you have already accepted the idea of a simplified last course. In any case, we suggest you try the following.

Example Strawberries

Never have we ever seen such strawberries as the ones in Japan. They were so lovely, plump and red. We could scarcely stand the thought of eating them, yet could not resist. And when we did, we felt as though we had never really tasted a strawberry before.

To serve strawberries in the manner of the Japanese, you must shop carefully, and preferably during the season. Their preparation is going to be hard to believe. Don't do a thing! That's right. Just wash in cool water and arrange on a small plate or platter. Select five or six ripe berries for each person and arrange as attractively as you know how.

You don't necessarily have to have all serving dishes alike. In Japan they are almost never the same, giving each diner a personal pleasure for just him alone. What a great way to use and enjoy some mix-match pieces of favorite old china.

As is the case throughout the world of good food, presentation is as important as the taste of the food itself. Using brightly-colored toothpicks as utensils, place the choice berries around a small flower blossom or use a brilliant-green maple or oak leaf as a sort of doily, contrasting with the strong red color of the berries. A sprig of mint, a small fresh stem of fir bough or parsley adds a touch worthy of contemplation by the diner.

We find that a just-washed berry, vine-ripened for natural goodness, is the most pleasing. Growing your own in an old barrel or wooden keg gives you the assurance of just picked freshness and with no worry about the possibility of having been sprayed with deadly chemicals. Don't spoil the effect by sprinkling with sugar in any form.

We promised you the "best of three worlds," and even though our Example Strawberries are surely one of the simplest delights of the Japanese, they are certainly among the best.

Simply Orange

Many times in Japan, something a bit sweet is served before the meal. Somehow, our Western tastes have managed to end the meal on a sweet note.

In Japan oranges are served very much like Example Strawberries. Each section is peeled to perfection and arranged on a pretty pottery plate, usually a darker color to show off the rich orange color of the fruit. The Japanese orange is somewhat smaller than our own and sectioned much in the same way as our tangerine. The closest in taste and appearance to our knowledge is the tangelo. They are not always plentiful, but are produced in good quantity and quality on the southernmost tropical islands of Shikoku and Kyushu.

To serve as the Japanese do, remove the peel and save to combine with fruit drinks in the blender. Arrange the orange sections on a plate, then dip lightly in pure, naturally produced orange-blossom honey. Now set in the sun if it is a nice day until they've dried a bit. If there is no sun, do this indoors for several hours before serving.

If we serve the tangelos fresh, they are slightly chilled, but not cold. As an accent, put one toasted almond near the arranged sections on each individual plate. A very small sprig of fresh mint leaves will add an additional color accent in true Japanese fashion.

If you can't find tangelos, use navel oranges, Valencias, or even good tangerines. The tangerines will prove less satisfactory, since they are so small and have seeds that must be removed. Ending the meal on such a light refreshing note is only surpassed by the fact that you've also had an excellent source of vitamin C.

Japanese or Chinese?

Generally we think of almond cookies as Chinese rather than Japanese. However, many times you will be served these little delights in a Japanese restaurant. Customs of food, dress and language indeed differ between the two races. Yet there are also many similarities.

We were fortunate enough to be in Osaka during a national holiday commemorating Adult's Day. This holiday is a large and important celebration honoring those Japanese who have reached their twentieth birthday during the year. Each such youth is officially recognized into formal adulthood on that day, the fifteenth of January.

Each new adult is presented with an exquisitely handsome china cup, to be used as a personal tea cup. Elaborately designed scenes of historical events are etched into the delicate china. We were told that the scenes were part of ancient Chinese legends. When we expressed some surprise at the intermingling of cultures and pressed for further explanation, our friend smiled and said, "Oh, our histories just seem to flow together somehow, so much so that it is difficult to know where one begins or the other ends." It is much the same with many Japanese and Chinese customs.

These cookies will freeze well.

Almond Cookies
ABOUT 6 DOZEN

4 cups unbleached flour

1 teaspoon baking powder

2 cups softened pure vegetable shortening

2 cups raw sugar

1 egg

1½ teaspoons almond extract

1 teaspoon vanilla

1 egg yolk

1 tablespoon water

blanched almonds

1 egg yolk, hard-boiled and sieved (optional)

Sift the flour and baking powder into a large bowl. Add the shortening and blend in the sugar, egg, almond extract and vanilla. Knead this mixture until thoroughly blended, then turn onto a floured pastry cloth. Lightly pat to a ¼-inch thickness. Cut with a round cookie cutter and place about 2 inches apart on an ungreased cookie sheet. Reshape remainder of dough and cut until all dough is used.

Combine the egg yolk and water and lightly brush the top of each cookie with this mixture. Place half a blanched almond in the center of each cookie, slightly pressing into the dough. Bake in a preheated 375°F. oven for 15 minutes, or until golden brown.

Variation   There is usually a secret to a special texture in foods. To get an authentic taste and texture to these almond cookies, hard cook an additional egg and put the yolk through a fine sieve, then add to the dough ingredients.

When melon is in season

Quarter the melon and scoop out the ball shape which is so popular. Make sure the melon is fully ripe but not overripe. Serve with a green garnish for cantaloupe, bright red blossoms for honeydew. Also chill slightly, definitely *not* until cold but just enough to produce the sensation of being covered with a cool, mountain dew.

To make this treat extra special for a party, try serving with glazed kumquats. The Japanese love celebrations and have many holidays.

Some Japanese sweets are very sweet and glazed kumquats are among their sweetest. This recipe works for other fruits, such as pineapple, grapes, cherries, and for nuts, too.

Glazed Kumquats
SERVES 4

kumquats

GLAZE
½ cup water
1 cup raw sugar

Wash fruit well and drain, then cover with fresh water. Cook only until tender, usually under 10 minutes. Remove and drain well, reserving the juices.

While the fruit is cooling, make the glaze by cooking the sugar and water mixture into a syrup. If using a candy thermometer, it is ready after reaching 140°F. If not, cook until a very firm ball forms when the syrup is dropped from a teaspoon into cool water. Add the fruit and simmer slowly for about 8 to 10 minutes. Drain and dust lightly with additional raw sugar.

The Japanese use sake or other wines. We prefer orange-flavored liqueur, adding a similar taste rather than another distinct flavor to confuse.

Mandarin Kabobs

Mandarin orange segments
verbena lemon leaves or mint leaves
Cointreau liqueur
sesame seeds

Arrange about 6 orange slices on a bamboo skewer alternating with lemon or mint leaves. Dip in the liqueur, then roll in sesame seeds. Serve only one skewer, with about six orange segments to each guest.

Sayonara

There are literally thousands of excellent Japanese foods that we could talk about here, but the recipes we've given you in this section constitute, in our estimate, the best. The springboard to almost all Japanese cuisine is contained in these selected recipes. Variations are your challenge.

The Old World—

Scandinavia

Notwithstanding the fact that much of the Old World has, through centuries of development, established excellent cuisines, we feel that the four countries that comprise Scandinavia exhibit a finer appreciation of the natural foods of the world.

Scandinavia is a vast sub-arctic region, bordered on the west by the Atlantic Ocean, on the north by the Arctic Ocean, the south by the Baltic Sea and on the east by the land masses of the Soviet Union. The four countries of Norway, Sweden, Finland and Denmark are inexorably tied together not only by geographical union, but also by historical and cultural similarities. Even so, there are distinct ethnic differences. Swedes are Swedes and proud of it. Danes are somewhat aloof and want no part of Finnish culture. Norwegians are very independent.

The fierce nature of the Vikings has undergone such a complete metamorphosis, that the peoples of Scandinavia today are the acknowledged leaders against violence in any form. Sweden is the home of the Nobel prize for peace. Finland takes no international political stand. Norway avoids any activity which would presume less than a total neutrality, and Denmark follows suit. Indeed, this new profile of resistance to human conflict is in sharp contrast to the warring Vikings of centuries past.

Television programming throughout Scandinavia is quiet. News commentators deliver the details of current events with a calm, soft-spoken delivery that makes news of an earthquake in Nicaragua or a train wreck in India sound more like an afternoon picnic than a major disaster. Dramatic programs exclude all violence, even anger. American films used on television are discreetly censored to delete what seems deplorable. This same attitude prevails in daily life.

For the visitor to Scandinavia, language barriers are virtually non-existent since almost everyone speaks English with a distinctly British accent. One might, however, be offended by what seems to be aloofness, at first exposure almost rude. This manner is not what it seems, but rather Scandinavian reserve. The peoples are warm and friendly when you get to know them, and their sincerity and true warmth are to be applauded.

Natural foods are a way of life in all Scandinavia: the fresher, the better; the more natural, the better. Deep ocean waters and thousands of clear fresh-water lakes supply abundant quantities of the fish so deeply appreciated in various forms as a mainstay of the diet.

The shallower waters of the numerous archipelagos yield good varieties of herring, but none so good as the Baltic herring, enjoyed by all Scandinavians at some time during each day, and all but revered by gourmets at any special occasion.

Although all of the Scandinavian countries resemble each other in many ways, customs and culture do vary to sizeable degrees. It seems, therefore, only just to examine the food habits and recipes of the individual countries that make up the lands of the Vikings.

Let us first examine Finland, easternmost partner of the group.

Finland With almost one-third of its land area lying above the Arctic Circle at the lines of parallel corresponding with those of Alaska, Finland is often presumed to be a land of severe cold, and so it is. However, the southernmost two-thirds of this land, larger than the British Isles, is persistently warmed by the ocean currents of the surrounding waters. A great deal of the time Helsinki is warmer in winter than most of central Europe, as much as forty degrees warmer, in fact. In contrast, the northern areas of Lapland are subject to months of almost total darkness and penetrating, bitter cold.

The old American axiom of "making hay while the sun shines" certainly applies to the agricultural aim of the industrious Finns. During the growing season, Finnish farmers work from before dawn until well past dusk to produce massive quantities of fresh produce. Their pride in quality is easily seen, for example, at produce bins in Helsinki harbor, where polished and precisely arranged vegetables await metropolitan shoppers. These farmers send members of the family down the waters of the archipelago in small boats laden with this produce, while they themselves toil in the fields to replenish the sold products.

Finnish housewives demand, and get, the freshest possible vegetables and fruits at this sprawling marketplace that opens early and closes promptly at two in the afternoon. Negotiating their trim boats back through the waters of the archipelago, the market-sellers return to attend to accumulated chores at the farms. They milk cows, press cheeses, clean and arrange vegetables for the following day. Theirs is a busy life.

Our visit to Finland began with the arrival at Helsinki harbor of our overnight steamship from Stockholm, Sweden. It was early in the morning and we were somewhat disappointed not to see the hundreds of farmers' boats scurrying into the harbor laden with their produce. As it turned out, the produce boats had arrived hours earlier, at first light, and by now had sold perhaps half of their products. We were soon impressed by what we saw.

Giant tender carrots, spinach, potatoes, leeks, cabbage and dozens of vine-ripened produce were expertly arranged in elevated bins. Beyond a doubt, this is natural food at its best, produced honestly by hard-working Finns, displayed with pride in immaculate stalls, and bought by appreciative housewives to serve the same day.

Oddly enough, during the lunch hour, we saw many Finnish men shopping with extreme care for various items. We later learned that the men do a great deal of the cooking. Lunching at Fazer's, Helsinki's fine lunchtime restaurant, we overheard several men describing their own, personally prepared evening meal of the night before. It is little wonder then that many of the fine Finnish recipes are attributed to male cooks. It cannot quite be labeled "hobby" cooking as we know it in the United States, which more or less becomes casual cooking by males, but rather a constant interest of Finnish men.

There is such a concern for food quality and good nutrition that Finland now has a Health Food Association. The Association has become the mentor for increased numbers of health food stores throughout Finland, featuring food supplements, organic produce and numerous specialty items to meet the current demand for healthier foodstuffs.

Throughout the world we find the "something to begin with" course. In the United States we have variations of the French hors d'oeuvres, Italians have antipasto, and the Scandinavians have Swedish *smorgasbord*, Norwegian *køltbørd*, Danish *smørrebrød* and Finnish *voileipäpöytä*. In every case, the Scandinavian buffet table features thinly sliced breads of many varieties, topped with an almost endless array of tasty morsels of meat, fish, fowl, cheese and condiments, anything in fact that complements the bread and butter base.

One of the finest reasons for serving the Scandinavian version of "something to begin with" is the enormous latitude available to the hostess or host. Whatever is available will usually work out very well.

The Finnish version usually has more fresh-water varieties of fish than its cousins and almost always contains the filled pastry, a specialty of Karelia in eastern Finland.

The Voileipäpöytä
(a buffet table)

The variety of foods in this course depends upon a different number of factors. How many guests will visit the table? How elaborate do you, as the hostess, wish the affair? What do you have on hand? What are the tastes of your guests? Are the items you want readily available?

In any case, the selection of breads is important as it is the basis for the buffet. Whole-grained breads, without preservatives, such as pumpernickel, whole-wheat, barley, rye and so on, are a must. Fresh, unsalted sweet-cream butter at just under room temperature (for easy spreading) will contribute a non-competitive taste base. Now we are ready to put something delicious on top.

According to your guests' tastes, have available:

    salt herring
    spiced herring

sardines
assorted cold cuts, sliced
  pork
  beef
  chicken
  smoked salmon

Add almost any other cold item you would like, including sour cream, and cheeses:

Swiss
cheddar
Edam
cottage

Authentically, bread, butter, meat, fish and cheese should be offered at the table first, followed by dishes such as:

casseroles
  meat and cabbage
  meat roast casserole
  potato
meat balls
roasts
egg dishes
salads

And finally, the desserts:

cakes
tortes
pastries
fruits

Beverages vary but should not be warm or hot. Cold milk or buttermilk, beer or fruit juices are appropriate. Coffee or hot tea follows the dessert course.

The *voileipäpöytä* may indeed be as simple or as elaborate as you choose. It is customary for guests to use fresh plates for each visit to the table; therefore be prepared for this demand.

Our first exposure to the *voileipäpöytä* occurred as passengers aboard the Silja Line steamship, a Finnish vessel making overnight connections between Stockholm and Helsinki. Entering the dining room we were immediately aware of a delicious aroma, and before us was the buffet table filled with a variety of simple and exotic dishes. We were never able to finish our exact count of the individual dishes on the long table, there were simply too many.

Watching our fellow passengers carefully, we noticed that everyone took only the cold dishes first, returning later for salads, meatballs, casseroles and similar fare. We did likewise, enjoying several return trips to the table.

To our surprise, a waitress approached and asked our order for the entree of our choice. Game hen, duckling, pork cutlet, chicken and veal were offered. Since we had generously satisfied ourselves at the *voileipäpöytä* we were at a loss to know how to order at that point. Discovering that we were Americans and new to the customs, our waitress was sensitive enough to recommend a tiny portion of each entree for us to discover without having to make a decision. She also elected a light Spanish rosé wine to accompany the dishes. So armed with this first experience at the *voileipäpöytä*, we then enjoyed every occasion.

Soups

Traditions and customs may vary a great deal throughout the world but soups seem to constitute a common bond. Through the use of varied techniques, available ingredients, herbs and spices, soups do have distinctive flavors that vary from country to country. The Finns have got to the heart of the matter.

This soup has a very delicate flavor and is the lacto-vegetarian's delight. If made properly it can only be enjoyed for a limited few weeks in midsummer. Most of the ingredients are very fresh young vegetables. We, however, enjoy this the year round, substituting available fresh vegetables and/or frozen ones with very good results. If you have a garden or access to one, you will never forget the sensation of freshness you will taste in this marvelous soup. If you don't have a garden, don't give up the idea of trying the recipe.

Kesäkeitto

1 cup sweet peas
1 cup green beans
cauliflower florets (1 small head)
4 to 6 tiny carrots, sliced
4 to 6 new potatoes, cubed (can use up to 2 cups)
4 to 6 new onions, diced
1 teaspoon sea salt
2 tablespoons butter
2 tablespoons unbleached flour
2 cups milk
1 teaspoon raw sugar
¼ teaspoon freshly ground white pepper
fresh parsley or fresh dill for garnish

Wash and prepare all the vegetables, handling them gently. Partially peel the potatoes, leaving some of the skin for flavor and texture. Barely cover the vegetables with water and add the salt. Cook quickly until just tender, about 5 minutes. Blend the butter, flour, milk, pepper and sugar and warm over low heat. Add to the vegetables. Simmer for about 10 minutes, or until thickened. Serve immediately, garnished with fresh parsley or a bit of fresh dill.

Variation For a more elegant version, use half milk and half cream.

Kesäkeitto Poaching Sauce

One summer afternoon we prepared a great deal more of this soup than we needed to satisfy our lunch guests. For dinner that evening we served filet of sole with the leftover *kesäkeitto* soup, which was now considererably thicker, ladled over the sole as a poaching sauce. A variety tray of sliced fresh fruit, black bread and butter, and chilled glasses of Chablis completed the menu.

We have never understood the American insistence on "hearty," "robust" or "man-pleasing" flavors for soups. Perhaps it's a holdover from pioneer days when strong flavors seemed to rejuvenate a man after hard labor.

If soup is the main course of a simple meal, perhaps a hearty flavor is necessary, but most often soup is used to prepare the taste buds for what is to follow. When that is the case, this is a great soup.

Use any combination of vegetables, but cabbage, turnips and artichokes are essential to the underlying flavor of this soup.

Vegetable Broth
(Kasvisliemi)

½ head small cabbage

2 cups chopped artichoke (either the edible flower or tubular roots sometimes referred to as Jerusalem artichokes. Finns use the latter.)

1 small turnip

1 small beet

½ cup green onions or leeks (if available)

1 medium brown onion

3 cups fresh peas in the pod (Chinese or unborn)

¼ cup carrot

4 medium stalks celery

½ cup radishes (I grow these all year in a window pot)

1 cup parsley

SPICE BAG
5 whole allspice

6 whole peppercorns

3 medium bay leaves

Wash and remove all stems and roots from the vegetable.

Pour about 3 quarts of water, seasoned with 2 teaspoons sea salt, over the vegetables. Put the spices into a mesh or cheesecloth bag: Drop the bag into the pot of vegetables and simmer 3 to 4 hours. Do not boil. Remove and discard the spice bag. Strain and serve the liquid as a bouillon. Use any remaining broth for seasoning. Finnish wives almost always have some in jars in the refrigerator.

Variation The following day place the saved vegetables in a casserole dish covered with cracker crumbs or toasted bread crumbs, top with sour cream and heat to piping hot in the oven.

We were a bit surprised at the interest shown by Finnish men when discussing foods, nutrition, and recipes. Many Finnish men are excellent cooks and are eager to share their culinary accomplishments with others. Our friend's husband prepares this special soup at their summer cottage out on the archipelago. It works equally as well on the stove at home or over an open fire, so try it the next time you go camping.

A Finn's Special Soup

2 quarts water, brought to a boil

4 potatoes, washed, peeled, and cut into pieces

1 spring onion, diced

several sprigs fresh dill

sea salt and white pepper to taste

¼ teaspoon allspice

2 pounds fresh fish (trout, perch, sea bass, salmon)

3 tablespoons butter

3 tablespoons unbleached flour

Put the first six ingredients into a large pot and simmer for about 40 minutes. Add the fresh fish that has been cleaned, deboned and cut into pieces. Cook until the fish is tender and flaky, about 10 minutes. Mix the butter and flour. Add a little of the cooking liquid and then add to the simmering soup. Cook until slightly thickened. Serve with black bread and sweet butter.

Our friend's husband floats chunks of the buttered bread in his soup. We also enjoyed this soup at the home of friends in Helsinki. That host, however, used milk rather than water as a liquid base for the soup and the result resembled a chowder. Another guest said that his version used tomatoes as well. It was agreed by all that a slight bit of lemon at serving time was an enhancement.

This is a beer soup and is quite unusual. It is delicious served alone, but may also be used as a type of fondue.

Kaljakeitto
SERVES 4

1 cup beer

2 teaspoons raw sugar

¼ teaspoon salt

2 tablespoons unbleached flour

2 cups milk

croutons (optional)

Let the beer stand until it is at room temperature. Add the sugar and salt. Warm on the stove. Mix the flour with a bit of the milk to make a paste, then gradually add the remaining milk. Heat the milk until a skin forms on top, then remove the skin. Using a wire whisk begin beating the milk mixture, gradually adding the beer mixture, and whipping until quite frothy. Serve at once.

The Finns serve this soup in individual bowls with croutons on top. We serve it in a large bowl placed in the center of the table along with a plate of cubed rye, black or sourdough bread. Spear the bread with fondue forks and dip in the soup.

Olavi Korvenpalo, president of the Health Food Association of Finland, was our host for lunch at Fazer's, in central Helsinki. We asked him to order something very Finnish and he was delighted to do so. The lunch was absolutely delicious and certainly "very Finnish." This recipe combines Olavi's efforts to describe it and our own kitchen trials and errors.

A Finnish Stroganoff
SERVES 2-4

½ teaspoon sea salt

¼ teaspoon white pepper

1 pound round steak (fresh ground by the butcher)

3 tablespoons sweet butter

1 small onion, finely chopped

½ cup water

¼ cup catsup

2 tablespoons unbleached flour

½ cup sour cream

¼ cup diced dill pickles

1 tablespoon sweet hot mustard

2 to 4 servings cooked brown rice

Lightly mix the salt and pepper with the ground round. Heat the butter in a skillet or dutch oven and brown the meat. Add the onion, catsup and ½ cup water. Cover and simmer slowly for at least 1 hour, stirring occasionally. Mix the flour with the sour cream. Stir in the pickles and mustard then add to the meat. Heat until piping hot then serve over the prepared brown rice. The nut-like flavor of the brown rice enhances the overall flavor. This is not only delicious but very nutritious. It is unfortunate that so many cooks use polished rice for this sort of dish, which has most of the good nutrition scrubbed off.

Another wonderful specialty at Fazer's is the mushroom sandwich, which we enjoyed immensely and although we did not get their recipe, we have worked with flavor and texture to the point that we are quite satisfied that we are enjoying a facsimile that would please anyone. We think the case for using the freshest of ingredients bears repeating, not only for the palate's sake, but for nutrition as well.

Mushroom Sandwich
(à la Fazer's)

2 to 3 tablespoons sweet butter

1½ cups fresh mushrooms sliced (save stems for soups)

¼ cup finely chopped white onion

1 cup raw cream

¼ teaspoon sea salt

¼ teaspoon white pepper

2 tablespoons unbleached flour

1½ slices of whole-grain bread per person

Brown the butter in a heavy skillet. Add the mushrooms and onion. Cook until just tender. Mix together and blend thoroughly the cream, salt, pepper and flour. Slowly add this sauce to the mushrooms. Stir and simmer until the sauce thickens. Toast the bread slices and butter with unsalted butter. Generously spoon the mushroom sauce over the toast points. Serve with a garnish of crab apples, sweet pickles and carrot sticks.

This lunch treat is very satisfying but not over-filling. It makes a marvelous brunch for Sunday mornings.

This stew is made in a large pot and slowly simmered all day long. Traditionally on baking days it sits on the edge of the wood stove, bubbling away without distracting the housewives occupied with breadmaking. On such days a dinner prepared with little effort is a blessing indeed. The stew is really more of a ragout as it is very thick. It may be made with chuck, sirloin, round steak, lamb or veal. A flavor similar to goulash results if you combine different varieties of meat.

Meat Stew
(Talonpoikaiskeitto)

3 tablespoons sweet butter

2 pounds of meat, cut into 1-inch cubes (chuck, sirloin, round steak, lamb or veal)

1 teaspoon sea salt

½ teaspoon white pepper

¼ teaspoon paprika

4 potatoes

4 carrots

4 small brown onions

Melt the butter in the bottom of the stewpot. Add the meat and season with salt, pepper, and paprika. Add the potatoes, then the carrots and onions. Cover tightly and cook slowly for 6 to 8 hours. Serve with whole-grain bread and sweet butter.

Variation Cook the stew in a preheated 250 °F. oven for about 7 hours. If it dries out too much, make a gravy from 2 tablespoons butter, 2 tablespoons flour and 1½ cups vegetable or beef broth.

The Finnish love of gamey tastes in fish, meat and fowl is illustrated in this traditional specialty. To most Finns, the gamier the better. Any small game bird may be used, such as quail, grouse, pheasant, squab or Rock Cornish game hen.

Braised Game Birds
(Paistettu Metsalintu)
SERVES 4

4 game birds

3 tablespoons butter

1½ teaspoons sea salt

fresh dill (optional)

3 tablespoons unbleached flour

2 cups water

¼ cup black currant jelly

Clean the birds and dry them with a paper towel. Melt the butter in a large skillet and brown the birds on all sides. Mix the salt and flour and rub on the outsides of the birds. (Some Finns place a bit of fresh dill inside the cavity for a subtle flavor.)

Place the birds breast up in the skillet and add 1 cup water. Bring to a boil, cover and reduce heat. Simmer for 30 minutes, add the remaining 1 cup water and continue cooking until the birds are tender, about 1 hour. Stir the currant jelly into the broth remaining in the pan and serve with the birds. Wild rice or a combination of wild and brown rice goes well with this treat.

Just as New England summers are filled with clambakes on the beach, so are Finland's summers the occasion for crayfish parties. Both the Swedes and the Finns claim to have originated the crayfish custom—the Finns say it is Finnish and the Swedes assert it is Swedish. Regardless of where it began, it is delicious! In most Scandinavian restaurants the crayfish are piled high on a huge platter. There need be no ceremony involved and nothing else need be served. Aquavit and beer are normally served with the meal and the tradition of a sip, then a bite, can be the cause of much merriment. The Finns also drink fresh buttermilk with these little flavor delights.

If you enjoy lobster, you will like crayfish. They are simple to prepare and delicious to eat. The crayfish available to us in the United States are found in a variety of freshwater locations, but predominantly in the northeast. They closely resemble the lobster, but are much smaller, usually 2½ to 3½ inches in length. The saltwater version is loosely referred to as the spiny lobster. If you live in a metropolitan area crayfish may be obtained from a fish market.

Most Scandinavians consume from 12 to 30 crayfish, but we would suggest 25 for 4 people the first time around. If you enjoy them, you can increase the number the next time.

Crayfish

25 crayfish

3 to 4 quarts water in a large pot

3 tablespoons sea salt

3 tablespoons dill seed

several bunches of fresh dill

The crayfish must be alive when purchased—make certain of this. Rinse the crayfish in cold water while boiling the water for cooking. Add the salt, dill seed, and 1 sprig of fresh dill to the boiling water. Boil for about 5 minutes to allow the flavor of the dill to permeate the water. Add the live crayfish, a few at a time, maintaining the water at the boiling point. When all the crayfish are in the pot, cover and cook for 5 to 8 minutes longer. Do not overcook for the sweet meat will toughen. (Like lobsters, they will turn a bright red.) When done, strain off the liquid and pile the crayfish onto a large deep dish. Place the remaining fresh dill around the sides. Pour the liquid into the dish.

The crayfish may be cooled to room temperature and served immediately or refrigerated for several hours until thoroughly chilled. Serve with a small dish or cup of melted sweet butter and fresh dill garnish.

As in lobster, the best meat is in the tail. The Finns clip off the claws, then split them vertically and dig out the meat and suck out the juices. The body itself contains no meat. The tail is cracked and separated in halves. Remove the meat and devein as with shrimp.

The eating process is a bit messy but this somehow adds to the fun of this bit of exotic dining. Here is a good place to borrow the Japanese custom of the *oshibori* (a hot wet cloth). Pass fingerbowls with a floating lemon slice to remove the juices and fish odor from the fingers.

This is one of the most famous fish preparations in all Finland. Tiny bony fish are baked in a rye dough. Although many of the younger generation Finns have neither the time nor inclination to prepare this popular dish, they still enjoy the flavor and anticipate the occasion to dine on kalakukko.

We adore good food, but also value our time. The following recipe will give you the old-world taste but with time-saving preparation.

Our Helsinki friend who gave us this recipe works full-time in the city and has two small children and a busy husband. She is a very liberated young lady but one who still respects her heritage. In fact, she tells me that her grandmother's original recipe for kalakukko *is kept side by side with her quicker version. Try it for a tasty treat.*

Kalakukko

1 large loaf rye or sourdough rye bread*

1 pound very small trout or smelts, cleaned and without heads or fins

6 slices bacon or ¼ pound salt pork

1 teaspoon sea salt

3 tablespoons butter

Slice the top third of the loaf lengthwise. Scoop out the bread in the remaining two-thirds, leaving about 1 inch of the bread. Fill this cavity with fish and bacon, adding the salt last. Let the filling mound up to the top. Scoop out part of the bread of the top third of the loaf. Replace the top of the loaf on the filled section and generously rub with the butter. Wrap in parchment paper and bake in a preheated 300 °F. oven for 3 hours. Remove from the oven and let stand for about 1 hour. Slice to serve.

If you are concerned about the tiny bones, be consoled by the fact that they seem to soften and disappear during the baking. An alternative is to use boned salmon.

*If available, use the darker Finnish rye for this recipe.

Blender Butter

The Finns enjoy this dish with generous amounts of melted or softened butter. Put 2 cups raw cream and ¼ teaspoon sea salt into the blender on low speed and blend until the butter is light and creamy. Or remove from the blender early and work the butter with a small wooden paddle, pouring off the liquid from time to time. Refrigerate or serve immediately with this quick version of *kalakukko*.

This delightful lady, speaking through an interpreter, told me of cooking for her family during the holidays many years ago. Her recipe for kalakukko *was so intriguing it was one of our first culinary experiments after returning to the United States.*

She didn't really give us any specific measurements, more the kinds of proportions that many good cooks describe as a "pinch" of this and a "pinch" of that. We were amused by the fact that language is no barrier between cooks whose gestures for the "pinch" are the same everywhere.

A Finnish Grandmother's Kalakukko

1 bread recipe, rye, sourdough rye, wheat or a blend

1 medium to small ham, weight 4 to 5 pounds (a good quality canned one is satisfactory)

½ cup mustard

½ cup raw or brown sugar (you may prefer honey)

In the case of a whole ham, trim fat, cook and remove bone. A canned ham should be cooked according to directions. Cool for at least 1 hour.

Prepare the bread recipe. Let it rise once and punch down. Roll out the dough so that it will amply cover the bottom and sides of a large baking pan or dutch oven with plenty of dough hanging over the sides. Place the cooled ham inside. Mix the mustard and sugar, then spread over the top of the ham. Bring up the sides of the bread dough and pinch closed over the entire ham, leaving one small opening to allow the steam to escape (this is important, otherwise the bread will be soggy). Bake in a preheated 375 °F. oven for 30 to 45 minutes, or until the bread is golden brown. Slice to serve. Cooked dried fruit is especially good as an accompaniment.

Part of the fun of this dish is to invite guests to reach over and pinch off bits of the outer crust, permeated with the ham and sugary-mustard flavor.

This dish can be served in a variety of ways—as an hors d'oeuvre, snack, canapé, sandwich or as a main course. The Finns enjoy strong flavors—pungent gravies, sour breads and gamey meats—so when preparing Finnish dishes, don't be afraid to add a bit of extra seasoning. Try this loaf first, then experiment with variations.

*Loaf
of Liver*

1 pound calf's liver

1 medium onion

¼ cup butter

2 eggs

½ cup raw cream

½ cup raw milk

1 to 4 finely chopped anchovies (optional)

⅓ cup dry bread crumbs

1 teaspoon sea salt

1 teaspoon raw sugar

1 teaspoon ground ginger

1 teaspoon seasoned pepper

¾ pound thinly sliced bacon

Have the butcher put the liver through a grinder or grind in a food grinder, using the fine blade. Finely chop the onion and sauté in the butter until golden and tender. Beat the eggs and the cream-milk mixture together, and add, stirring constantly. Add the remaining ingredients, except for the liver and bacon, and blend thoroughly. Add the liver and blend thoroughly (a blender will speed up this process).

Preheat the oven to 325 °F. Line a bread or loaf pan with the bacon, covering the entire surface and leaving the ends hanging over the top. Pour in the liver mixture and fold the bacon ends over. Place a piece of heavy baking parchment over the top and secure with a piece of twine. Place the bread pan in a larger shallow pan and pour water into the outer pan to come up several inches on the bread pan. Bake for about 1½ hours, or until very firm. Remove the parchment and cool. When cool, remove from the pan and store in refrigerator.

This is delicious as a main course with mushroom sauce (see **Mushroom sandwich**) spooned over the liver loaf slices.

For use at the Finnish *voileipäpöytä* or buffet table, spread on crackers or thinly sliced rye bread. For one highly successful dinner party, we made the liver loaves in four diminutive bread pans and placed one at each corner of the buffet table.

Variations   Use 4 small filets of beef, ground round patties, or soybean patties. Cut pieces of toast to fit the meat. Spread the toast with the liver loaf or use a thin slice. Broil the meat to medium rare for full flavor. Place on the toast and spoon mushroom sauce over it.

Spread the top of a slice of liver loaf with **Egg butter.**

The Finns use this spread over filled meat or rice pastries as well as with cold meat dishes.

Egg Butter

½ cup butter, softened
¼ teaspoon sea salt
1 hard-cooked egg, finely chopped
    sprig of fresh dill (optional)

Whip the butter until light and fluffy. Add the salt and egg. Put into the blender and puree.

An optional addition of a small sprig of fresh dill makes this delicious spread authentically Finnish. Use wherever you use butter as a spread.

In Finland a favorite pastime in the spring and summer is to walk through the woods gathering the varieties of dark brown mushrooms just before dinner. There is a lovely, earthy, woodsy smell to a freshly-picked basket of these most delicious of the fungi. In your own market, select the freshest possible. This is a pungent-flavored salad, and one that is unusual.

Fresh Mushroom Salad

4 cups lettuce of your choice (a blend is nice)
1 pound fresh mushrooms
    juice of ½ lemon
2 tablespoons grated sweet onion
½ teaspoon coarse salt
¼ teaspoon white pepper
1 tablespoon raw sugar
¼ cup raw heavy cream

Shred the lettuce and set in the refrigerator to chill. Bring 2 cups water to the boil. Wash and slice the mushrooms, then drop into the boiling water. Cover and immediately remove from the fire. Let stand for 1 minute. Rinse in cold water, drain, and pat dry with paper towels. Spoon about 2 teaspoons of the lemon juice over the mushrooms in a bowl. Add the onion, salt, pepper, sugar and cream. Mix well, cover, and set in the refrigerator until serving time. Serve on the lettuce.

Cucumbers are served as a salad in Finland much in the same fashion as lettuce salads are served in the United States. Many times they are simply sliced and served with a dash of salt and a sprig of fresh dill. Here's a more elaborate version.

Cucumber Salad

2 cucumbers
1 teaspoon dried or fresh dill
   sea salt and white pepper to taste
1 tablespoon raw sugar
¼ cup white wine vinegar
1 tablespoon polyunsaturated salad oil
¼ cup water

Slice the cucumbers thinly and place on a large flat dish. Sprinkle with the dill, salt and pepper. Sprinkle the sugar evenly on top. Combine the vinegar, salad oil and water. Blend thoroughly and ladle over the cucumber slices. Cover and refrigerate until thoroughly chilled.

Variation   Add 1 small chopped apple and ½ cup sour cream to the above dressing. Sliced tomatoes will add color as well as enhance the flavor and nutrition.

This recipe is included mostly for fun. We don't think it is something you will want to do often, but it is interesting and truly Finnish.
   This bread sometimes turns rather brick-like in consistency instead of crisp like a cracker. Occasionally it becomes so hard it should not be bitten with the front teeth for fear of fracturing a tooth. However, once a small piece is in your mouth it is quite tasty.
   Since the Finnish weather doesn't allow for year-round vegetable production, the Finns have traditionally enjoyed the extra crisp texture of this bread as a good substitute for roughage in the diet.
   During the time Finns baked only once or twice a year, these breads were hung on long poles from the ceiling. If you are decorating a corner of a room in your home with historical memorabilia, try hanging a dozen of these round, thin breads with a hole in the center.

Finnish Hardtack

1 cake yeast or 1 tablespoon yeast granules
2 cups warm water
1 teaspoon salt
4 cups rye flour (approximate)

In a warm bowl dissolve the yeast in 2 cups water until it bubbles. Sift the salt into the rye flour and combine with yeast water. Mix well. Cover with a slightly damp towel and let rise in a warm place until doubled in bulk. Punch down and form into balls 3 inches in diameter. Use flour to prevent dough from sticking to your hands. Roll each ball out into a round, about ¼ inch thick. Using a large spatula, lay each round out on a greased or teflon-surfaced cookie sheet. Cut a 2-inch diameter hole in the center of each round. Let rise about 30 minutes. Prick the top generously with the tines of a fork. Bake quickly in a preheated 450 °F. oven for about 10 minutes.

You will want the rounds to be firm, but bendable when removed from the oven. Finnish housewives hang these rounds so they dry by themselves. We dry them by returning to a cool oven overnight. The next morning they are ready to eat.

Although we had made hardtack many times before, we decided to make some again while writing this section of the book. The same evening, we were invited for an impromptu dinner at friends. We took along several rounds of the still warm hardtack as a conversation piece. Our hosts were anxious to try a bit and as dinner was served, we all pinched off bits of the still pliable rounds. They were absolutely delicious with sweet-cream butter smeared generously on each morsel.

Decide to make this bread at least two days in advance as the sour taste comes from a sour starter.

Sour Starter

Make the sour starter as follows: mix ½ cup rye flour with ½ cup skim milk in a small bowl. Cover with plastic wrap and let stand in a warm place until it becomes bubbly and has a definite sour odor. If a crusty layer has formed, remove before using the starter. If the mixture has developed a fully soured odor and you are not ready to make the bread, store, covered, in the refrigerator until ready to use.

Sour Rye Bread
3 LOAVES

2 to 3 tablespoons cornmeal

3½ cups rye flour

1 package yeast or 1 tablespoon dry yeast granules

¼ cup warm water

2 cups lukewarm skim milk

2 teaspoons salt

1 tablespoon raw sugar

2 tablespoons butter

2½ cups unbleached wheat flour

Set out a small dish with the cornmeal mixed with ½ cup of the rye flour to be used later.

In a large warmed bowl dissolve the yeast in the warm water. When bubbling, add the milk, salt, sugar and butter. Add half of the rye flour and beat vigorously. Add the sour starter. Mix well, cover, and let rest for 5 minutes. Add the remaining wheat flour and mix well until a stiff dough forms. Cover, and let rest for 10 minutes. Place in a large buttered bowl, turning once so the buttered side is up. Cover with a damp cloth and let rise in a warm place until doubled in bulk. Punch down, kneading slightly, then divide into three equal portions. Sprinkle about half the cornmeal-flour mixture onto a pastry cloth and shape the dough into 3 round loaves (the cornmeal gives a nice texture to the loaves). Lightly butter 3 round cakepans or cookie sheets. Prick the loaves generously with the tines of a fork. Bake in a preheated 375°F. oven for 40 to 50 minutes. Cool on wire racks after rubbing the tops of the loaves with butter.

This bread may be baked in two loaves rather than three. It may be kept for several days and served toasted.

The Finns use sour cream in many recipes from toppings to pastries. This sour cream cake is delicious, much like a moist pound cake. It is usually served un-iced at the Finnish coffee table. If you are invited for coffee there is a table laden with cookies, cakes and the like. With each cup of coffee or tea, the guest is expected to sample a different sweet.

Un-iced
Sour Cream
Cake

3 eggs
1½ cups raw sugar
1½ cups sour cream
¼ teaspoon almond flavoring
½ teaspoon vanilla
2½ cups unbleached flour, sifted before measuring
1 teaspoon baking powder
½ teaspoon sea salt
½ teaspoon cinnamon
½ teaspoon cardamom (ginger may be substituted)
½ cup sifted confectioner's sugar

Beat the eggs with an electric beater until light and fluffy, adding the sugar gradually. Fold in the sour cream and flavorings. Sift dry ingredients together (except for the confectioner's sugar), add to the liquid, and mix well. Grease a tube pan with butter and dust lightly with a combination of 2 tablespoons flour and 2 tablespoons confectioner's sugar. Turn the pan upside down above the sink and tap sharply to release excess flour-sugar coating. Pour in the batter and bake in a preheated 325 °F. oven for about 45 minutes. The cake is done when a toothpick comes out clean. Let cook in the pan for about 10 minutes before removing, then dust with the remaining confectioner's sugar.

For variety whip ½ cup raw cream and gently fold this into ¼ to ½ cup sour cream. Top with a dash of cinnamon and serve on the side.

Our family loves this cake served warm with a bit of homemade jam or fresh strawberries.

In Finland, this pudding is usually made with lingonberry juice. We use fresh organic cranberry juice. You may substitute any other juice you prefer. This recipe is for a tart juice, so if you use a sweeter one, such as raspberry or strawberry, add 1 tablespoon lemon juice before cooking to give additional tartness.

Whipped
Berry
Pudding

3 cups organic juice
½ cup raw sugar (less 1 tablespoon)
½ cup cooked cream of wheat

Bring the juice to a boil, then add the sugar gradually, stirring constantly. When boiling resumes, slowly add the cream of wheat. Stir as often as necessary to prevent sticking. Reduce the heat and simmer 8 to 10 minutes, or until the mixture thickens. Remove from the fire and pour into a large mixing bowl. Beat at high speed with an electric mixer for about 15 minutes. The mixture will triple in volume, become light in color, and very fluffy in texture. A Finnish friend tells us that in the old days the pudding may have been beaten by hand for as long as an hour. This delightful pudding is served in individual bowls at room temperature. It may be very, very slightly chilled, but the flavor is most distinct at room temperature.

For a festive occasion serve this light dessert topped with whipped cream and ladle a teaspoon of Marsala wine or a fruity liqueur on top.

The Finns serve these snows at room temperature. Any leftovers are frozen and served later as an ice—a very refreshing summertime dessert.

Finnish Snow

4 egg whites
½ cup sugar

Beat the egg whites until stiff. Gradually add the sugar and beat until stiff peaks form. Serve immediately, or chill or freeze.

Strawberry Variation   Wash, drain thoroughly and dry 2 cups strawberries (if using frozen, drain off all juice). Put the berries through a sieve. Fold the resulting puree very lightly into the egg white mixture. Whip 1 cup raw cream and fold into the berry mixture. Serve in individual small dishes.

Raspberry Variation   If the raspberries are fresh sweeten with ¼ cup raw sugar. Sieve and proceed as with Strawberry Snow.

Apple Variation   This variation calls for 2 cups cooled homemade applesauce. Make this like the other variations, omitting the whipped cream. Top with a dash of cinnamon.

Norway   The deep fjords of Norway are magnificently carved into an overwhelming backdrop of high mountains, deep forests and an enormously clear sky. Like the other countries of Scandinavia, Norway is exposed to a range of climate from bitter arctic cold to warm, mild winters. Because of the proximity of the Gulf Stream, the southernmost portion is generally warmer in winter than Sweden.

Surrounded by more than 12,000 miles of ocean coastline, it is no wonder that fish plays an important part in human nutrition there. The Norwegian fishing fleet has long been the envy of many countries whose appreciation of that delectable ocean produce has outrun the ability to catch sufficient quantities. This expertise has given Norway an expanding trade prospectus for hundreds of food items and manufactured goods which they are not equipped to produce, either through lack of technological advantage or inadequate agricultural output.

For centuries Norwegian ships have sailed southward to France, the Mediterranean and the Near East with bulging holds of fish, to return months later loaded with grains, olives, wines and manufactured goods obtained in exchange for their fish.

Viewing the sprawling topography of Norway from the air, one would be hard-pressed to imagine much of the mountainous jumble as being suited for agriculture. The observation would be nearly true, for probably less than 5 percent is arable and even less is actually used. Nevertheless, Norwegians are proud of their independence in producing most of their foodstuffs. Between the seas, the mountain slopes and the sparse meadows, they have wrung great volumes of some of the finest, most natural and certainly the freshest foods imaginable.

Cabbages, some almost a foot in diameter, apples that seem to have a distinctly finer character and a variety of other produce grow in an abundance in this cool climate where, during summer, the sun shines almost around the clock.

Patient Norwegians toil from early until late on the grassy slopes of small farms contiguous to the great fjords, as yet unexposed to the atmospheric pollution from Central Europe. Nevertheless, Norwegians are watching with keen interest the threat to their agricultural safety.

Our own first look at Norway began as we crossed the border station between Sweden and the gently rolling hills of eastern Norway by car.

As we did so, we reflected back some years ago to the first driving tour across the United States with our children, recalling that our son David observed with a degree of disbelief, as we entered Tennessee from Arkansas, "Humph . . . doesn't look any different to me!" And so it is upon entering Norway, but as the miles roll by on the way to Oslo, a change takes place that puts the topography into perspective. It is a land of intense beauty.

The Norwegian køltbørd

The Norwegian answer to the "something to begin with" course bears a marked resemblance to that of the other Scandinavian countries, except for a few interesting variations.

It seems to us that generally there are fewer items and a greater variety of fish. This may give some credence to the Swedish accusation that "the Norwegians only eat fish," but on the other hand it may well be that the Norwegians simply have more varieties of fish than their neighbors. In either case the *køltbørd* is a delicious way to start any meal in Norway, or in your home.

Also featured on the *køltbørd* table are exotic smoked partridge, grouse and reindeer. The latter come in good supply from the colder northern regions where there are great herds of reindeer cared for much the same way as Angus cattle in the Southwest of the United States.

Other specialties of the table include eel, both smoked and pickled, herring, cod and the delicious sardines. Bread takes many forms and since the dairying industry produces an abundance of butter and fine cheeses, they are found on the table too.

During holidays, festivals and weddings we have found the *køltbørd* to be more elaborate, and for good reason, for after all, such events *are* special occasions and deserve more attention.

Use any or all of the following:

> herring (pickled or smoked)
> sardines
> smoked fish of any variety you like
> anchovies

pickled vegetables (beets, cauliflower, onions, beans)
cheeses (any aged variety)
smoked venison chips (cold)
smoked lamb cutlets (cold)
any cold meats (in thin slices)

Also serve:

lettuce
cucumbers
onion slices
parsley
fresh dill

a variety of fresh whole-grained breads, sliced,
and very thin, crispy rye crackers

chilled aquavit, beer, milk, Spanish wine

The Norwegians lay out the *kφltbφrd* as attractively as possible, and invite the guests to return to the table again and again. It is a good time for conversation and sensitizing the palate for the soups and entrees to follow.

The elaborate nature of Scandinavian *smorgasbord, smφrrebrφd, voileipäpöytä* or *kφltbφrd* can somewhat overwhelm Americans; the number and variety of foods seem overabundant in terms of our own dining standards. We urge you not to regard the buffet table with alarm, but to approach with selectivity. Eat only things that most appeal to you and only in amounts compatible with your taste and comfort. Even though we have cautiously approached a *kφltbφrd* groaning under as many as fifty individual dishes, we have somehow managed to taste more than half of them.

After tantalizing your guests' taste buds with the *kφltbφrd,* serve the soup.

Norwegian soups are among the best—possibly because they use only the freshest of ingredients. The demand for natural foods is a way of life there. So let it be with you, if you care to emulate these healthy souls.

This is a Norwegian favorite. If you have a spinach-hater in your family use this soup to break the habit. If you don't tell them it's spinach, they may not figure it out until they've fallen in love with the flavor. They may inquire about the dark green color. In that case just tell them "it's a surprise" and see if that will hold them off until after they've tasted it.

Spinatsuppe
(Norwegian Spinach Soup)

1 pound fresh spinach, or 1 package frozen
(fresh is best, of course)

1 quart chicken stock or broth

   sea salt and white pepper to taste

2 tablespoons butter

2 tablespoons unbleached flour

1 or 2 hard-cooked eggs
(thinly sliced or coarsely grated)

Cook the spinach until just done in the chicken stock with salt and pepper. Drain off the juices and save. Chop the spinach finely. In a small bowl mix the butter and flour into a paste. Add a bit of the stock to make a smooth thin liquid. Warm the reserved juices, then over a low heat add the butter-flour mixture slowly, stirring with a wire whisk until smooth. Add the spinach and simmer for 5 minutes. Serve immediately with the egg garnish.

Quick Spinach Soup

This variation, developed by accident, pleases our family and guests just as much as the authentic version just given.

To 1 quart of water add 1 tablespoon chicken bouillon powder and simmer until the bouillon powder is completely dissolved. Season with salt and pepper and put into the blender with leftover spinach. Puree for 1 minute, then quickly return to the pot to simmer. Combine 1 tablespoon flour and 1 tablespoon butter and add a small amount of the simmering broth. Stir into the soup to thicken. Serve garnished with hard-cooked egg. Whole-grained bread, butter, apple wedges, and Edam cheese complete the menu.

   We love all the soups of Norway. We have found we have something in common with Norwegian housewives. Many times we make a meal of soup and nice warm bread and that's virtually it except perhaps for a little wine and fruit. This is one of our favorites.

This delicious and nutritious, natural-flavored soup will make a hearty meal or an excellent bridge between the kφltbφrd and entrees of a more elaborate dinner.

Cauliflower Soup

1 medium to large head cauliflower, very fresh

1 quart water or chicken stock

1 teaspoon sea salt

¼ teaspoon white pepper

1 teaspoon grated onion (optional but very good)

1 egg yolk

1 cup light cream or half and half

3 tablespoons butter

1 tablespoon finely chopped parsley heads

Cut the cauliflower into smallish pieces. Cook in the water with salt, pepper and onion. If desired for decoration, cut several florets whole and cook until just done, then remove and chill to hold shape. Continue cooking the remainder of the cauliflower until very tender. Put the cauliflower into a blender with part of the liquid and puree. If you don't have a blender, use the back of a wooden spoon and force through a sieve or vegetable strainer. Return to the pot with the remaining liquid.

Beat the egg yolk with a wire whisk until light in color and blend with the cream. Gradually add 3 or 4 tablespoons of the simmering liquid to the egg mixture, beating with the whisk. Then add all to the pot and simmer until smooth and thickened. Add the butter and simmer for about 10 minutes.

Bring the refrigerated cauliflower florets to room temperature. Place one floret into the bottom of each individual serving bowl, pour in the soup, and top with a little parsley.

Every cuisine has done its share of borrowing. Although this soup was served in the main dining room of the Continental Hotel in Oslo, and appropriately listed on the menu as French Onion Soup, we feel it has been thoroughly "Norwegianized." It is another of our family's favorites.

*French
Onion
Soup*
SERVES 4

¼ cup butter

3 medium or 2 large onions, peeled and thinly sliced

1 quart beef broth or soup stock*

1 bay leaf

¼ teaspoon freshly ground pepper

4 thick slices French bread

4 tablespoons grated Parmesan cheese

4 thin slices Gruyere cheese

Melt the butter and add the onion slices. Sauté very slowly until golden brown. (This process cannot be hurried or the onion will develop a burnt taste and ruin the delicate flavor of this soup.) When properly browned, add the stock then the bay leaf and other seasonings. Simmer for about 30 minutes, remove the bay leaf, and prepare to serve in individual ovenproof bowls. Preheat the oven to 400 °F. Cut the bread slices to fit the bowls, top with cheese, and place on a cookie sheet in the broiler until the cheese has melted. Pour the soup into the bowls, then carefully set the cheese-covered bread slice into the hot soup. Serve immediately.

Variation The addition of a spoonful of whipped cream or sour cream is a variation the Norwegians would approve.

*Soup stock can be made by boiling 1 quart water with salt and pepper to taste, 2 stalks cut up celery and 1 soup bone or veal knuckle. Cover and simmer for about an hour. Strain and use.

Although this Norwegian favorite resembles a bouillabaisse in many respects, we don't really believe it is borrowed from the French, but rather is the pure invention of taste-conscious Norwegians with an abundant supply of good fish. This recipe is more a stew than a soup and may be varied in many ways.

If you have fresh halibut, cod, haddock or white fish you may employ the Norwegian practice of making the soup stock by simmering the head, fins and tail in 1 quart water until thoroughly flavored, and then discard the fish parts. Or you can simmer the cleaned fish in 1 quart water until almost tender and then remove. Use about 1 pound of fish.

Fish	1 teaspoon salt
Soup	¼ teaspoon freshly ground pepper
	1 bay leaf
	1 stalk celery
	½ cup chopped onion
	¼ teaspoon freshly chopped dill
	1 potato peeled and cut into small pieces
	¼ cup finely chopped carrots
	¼ cup finely chopped parsnips or turnip
	1 tablespoon chives
	1 egg yolk
	⅓ cup sour cream
	½ cup milk

Add the first 6 ingredients to the 1 quart fish stock. Simmer slowly for about 45 minutes and strain. Add the fish, cut into larger than bite-sized pieces, to the strained stock along with the potato, carrots, parsnips and chives. Cook until the fish is tender. Remove the fish and reserve. Mix the egg yolk, sour cream and milk and add a little of the hot stock, stirring with a wire whisk. Slowly add to the soup to thicken. Simmer very slowly for about 10 minutes, being careful not to let it boil. Return the reserved fish and reheat.

Serve in good-sized bowls. Garnish with a small spoonful of sour cream and sprinkle with fresh parsley and dill. Pass Scandinavian crisp bread or flat bread and sweet-cream butter. Most health food stores now carry several varieties of flat bread.

Oh, if it were true in America!

Recalling happy experiences in Norway reminds us of a fact that astounded us as we first visited the fish markets of Oslo harbor. That fact is that there was no overbearing odor of fish. The reason, we were told, is that Norwegians, by tradition, insist on the freshest of everything! And this goes especially for fish.

Most fish is brought to the marketplace alive, still swimming in large tanks taken from the vessels. It isn't an uncommon sight to see a Norwegian housewife point to a swimming fish in a market tank, purchase it, and scurry home to cook it. The Norwegian housewife is insistent in her demand for the freshest of the fresh.

Salads in Norway are quite different from American ones. Crisp lettuce is almost a rarity. Instead, cucumbers (plain, pickled, marinated or in sour cream), radishes, tomatoes, mushrooms, cauliflower, carrots, peas and so on, function as the "salad." Here is an unusual and tasty cucumber combination.

Cucumber and Apple Salad

1 cucumber, cut in bite-sized pieces

2 apples, cut in bite-sized pieces

2 teaspoons raw sugar

½ teaspoon salt

¼ teaspoon paprika

Combine the ingredients and serve on a large lettuce or cabbage leaf with sour cream.

This is a marvelous luncheon dish.

Fish Salad

2 cups cooked fish, deboned and flaked

1 cup sour cream

1 tablespoon grated horseradish

1 cup grated sweet onion

1 tablespoon lemon juice

1 tablespoon chopped fresh dill

1 teaspoon salt

¼ teaspoon white pepper

1 hard-cooked egg

Mix the ingredients except the egg together gently so as to not break up the fish flakes too much. Cover and chill in the refrigerator for about 1 hour. Serve, mounded on shredded lettuce or a combination of shredded cabbage and lettuce. Grate the egg on top and if you have developed a liking for dill, sprinkle a bit more on top. Serve with crisp-bread crackers with sweet butter or soft, spreadable cheese. Cold buttermilk, beer, or chilled herb tea with a bit of mint are good accompaniments.

This is a Norwegian favorite. Use the freshest mackerel available and marinate for a unique flavor.

Marinert Makrel
(marinated grilled mackerel)

4 medium-sized fresh mackerel

3 tablespoons lemon juice

1 teaspoon sea salt

    freshly ground black pepper

5 tablespoons olive oil

5 tablespoons chopped onion

4 tablespoons polyunsaturated salad oil

4 tablespoons melted sweet butter

Have the backbones removed from the mackerel and place the fish in a shallow baking dish. Combine the lemon juice, salt, pepper, olive oil and chopped onion into a marinade. Coat the fish thoroughly. After 30 minutes turn the fish to marinate the other side (do not marinate for more than 1 hour). Preheat broiler. Combine the oil and butter and coat the broiler pan to prevent sticking. Broil the fish, basting occasionally. Brush on any remaining oil-butter mixture at serving time.

Fish puddings are a household word in Norway. There are many varieties as each housewife will vary the ingredients. This pudding is very light in texture, much like a soufflé. It is as unusual in taste as in texture.

Fish Pudding

¼ cup bread or cracker crumbs (optional)

2 pounds fresh fish (haddock, cod, sea bass or similar)

½ cup light cream

½ cup butter

2 eggs, separated

1 teaspoon sea salt

¼ teaspoon white pepper

⅛ teaspoon cardamon or nutmeg (optional)

1 tablespoon cornstarch

1 tablespoon unbleached flour

1 cup heavy cream (certified raw is best)

Grease a mold pan or loaf pan (1½ or 2 quart size). If you use the cracker or bread crumbs, sprinkle until the pan is evenly coated. Tap the pan to remove excess.

Clean the fish, remove bones and skin, and cut into small pieces. Put a few pieces of fish and a little of the cream into a blender. Puree (it only takes a few seconds). Pour into a mixing bowl. Repeat until all fish and light cream are pureed. (If you don't have a blender, put the fish through a meat grinder several times and blend with the light cream until smooth.) Melt the butter and cool. Add to the fish mixture.

Beat the egg yolks until light in color and mix with the fish. Add the spices, cornstarch, and flour. Preheat the oven to 325 °F. Whip the cream, then the egg whites. Fold together with fish mixture. Pour into the pan to three-fourths full. Cover with foil. Set into a larger pan and set into oven. Pour boiling water into the outer pan to about half way up the sides of the baking pan. Cook approximately 1 hour, or until a toothpick comes out clean. The cooking time is variable from 50 minutes to 1¼ hours so watch it carefully. Overcooking will not help this delicacy. Unmold by placing platter on top of the pan and invert quickly. Serve with hot melted butter, **Shrimp** or **Mushroom sauce.**

This is also delicious served thinly sliced on an open-faced sandwich with a tiny pink shrimp as garnish.

Fish Ball Variation

Follow the directions for **Fish pudding** (see above) except for pouring into pan. Chill the entire mixture for about 1 hour, then shape into small balls (about 1 inch in diameter). Cook by gently dropping the balls into 4 or 5 inches of simmering salted water. Cook until firm, about 2 to 4 minutes.

Fish balls are delicious with shrimp sauce or served cold as an hors d'oeuvre.

Shrimp Sauce

2 tablespoons butter

2 tablespoons unbleached flour

    salt and pepper to taste

1½ cups milk

2 cups cooked shrimp, deveined

Melt butter over low heat. Stir in flour and seasonings. Using a wire whisk, blend in the milk, stirring until thick and creamy. Add the shrimp and heat thoroughly. Ladle generously over the hot fish pudding or the fish balls or pass separately in a gravy boat.

Variation Substitute 2 cups sliced mushrooms for the shrimp.

Fish au Naturel

The Norwegians, loving fish as they do, serve it sautéed, boiled, broiled or poached. In any case, the fish is very fresh. Use butter, salt, pepper and cook by any favorite method until just tender. Sauces are usually melted butter (sweet cream) mixed with dill, parsley or sour cream. Occasionally the butter is whipped with lemon juice, horseradish and hard-cooked egg, then chilled to serve with fish, hot or cold.

Example
Trout
SERVES 4

4 freshly caught trout (the Norwegians leave head and tail intact)

salt and pepper to taste

⅓ cup unbleached flour

½ cup butter

1 cup sour cream

1 teaspoon lemon juice

2 tablespoons chopped parsley

Clean the trout, rinse sparingly with cold water and pat dry. Season the insides with salt and pepper. Mix the flour with additional salt and pepper and coat both sides of the fish. Melt 2 tablespoons butter in a cast-iron skillet. Sauté the trout for about 5 minutes on each side. Remove to warm oven. Add the remainder of the butter to the skillet with the sour cream and blend thoroughly. Add the lemon juice and the parsley. Ladle the sauce over the cooked trout. Use this preparation with virtually any fish of your choice.

Meat

Beef cattle are rarely raised in Norway because the terrain and suitable feedstuffs are not available. Because of this, the Norwegians have not developed a taste for beef. A limited supply of beef from slaughtered milk cows is available, although very inferior to the range beef of the United States. For this reason beef is subordinate to the use of sheep and reindeer.

The rugged mountain slopes *are* very well-suited for sheep and goats who scour the hillsides and low valleys for a variety of edible wild plants and scrub growth. The goats are milked, rendering a fine selection of good cheeses. The sheep are slaughtered for excellent mutton and young lamb.

In the colder Arctic regions reindeer roam in herds tended by the nomadic Lapps and are the source of the tasty reindeer cutlets and gamier-tasting red meats popular with Norwegians.

In many ways we compare this to our version of the "New England Boiled Dinner."

Lamb and Cabbage Dinner

2 tablespoons butter

2 pounds lamb shoulder, cut in 1-inch cubes

  sea salt and pepper to taste

1 tablespoon lemon juice

1 onion, thinly sliced

1 cup chopped parsley

1 head firm cabbage

In a large Dutch oven melt the butter and quickly brown the lamb cubes. Add enough water to completely cover the lamb, about 2 cups. Season with salt, pepper and lemon juice. Cover and put into a pre-heated 325 °F. oven for about 45 minutes. Add the onion and then the parsley. Cut the cabbage head into 8 wedges and add to the pot. Continue baking, covered, for an additional 45 minutes. Serve with boiled or steamed potatoes.

This recipe lends itself readily to experimentation. Vegetables such as carrots or celery may be added, and Norwegian cooks occasionally add sour cream.

This is a very popular dish throughout Norway.

Baked Lamb

1 medium leg of lamb or chops or shanks
2 tablespoons butter
    salt and pepper to taste
½ teaspoon paprika
1 tablespoon vinegar
1 cup sour cream

Brown the lamb in butter, then place in a buttered baking pan or ovenproof dish. Combine the salt, pepper, paprika, vinegar and sour cream and pour over the lamb. Cover and bake in a preheated 325 °F. oven until tender, about 1-1½ hours. Serve with boiled potatoes or brown rice.

We sometimes have over-active imaginations. When we saw this delicacy on the menu in a Norwegian restaurant, all we could think of were Santa's reindeer—Donner, Blitzen and the whole gang, right down to Rudolph. However, the cutlets were delicious. The nearest comparable taste to be found in the United States is venison, which has a strong pungent flavor. If you prefer a milder, less gamey taste, mix 1 cup water with 1 cup vinegar and soak the meat in this solution for about 2 hours. Pat the meat dry and proceed with this recipe.

Reindeer Cutlets
SERVES 4

1 clove garlic
1 tablespoon butter
  sea salt and pepper to taste
4 venison steaks, chops, or flanks
1 onion
1 carrot
1 cup water
1 tablespoon lemon juice
1 tablespoon parsley
½ cup sour cream

Rub the garlic clove over the bottom of a cast-iron skillet. Squeeze with a garlic press and discard the remaining clove. Melt the butter in this skillet. Salt and pepper the meat, then sear on both sides until well browned. Turn off the fire. Add to the skillet the onion, cut in half, the carrot, cut into several pieces, water, lemon juice and parsley. Cover and bake in a preheated 300 °F. oven for about 1 hour, or until the reindeer is tender (cooking time really depends on the cut and size). Remove the meat and keep warm. Add the sour cream to the pan juices and cook until thoroughly heated. Serve over the meat.

Variation   Use half water and half Burgundy wine to cook the meat. Add ¼ cup raw goat cheese with the sour cream. Serve with a tart jelly such as lingonberry, currant or cranberry. Wild rice is an excellent accompaniment.

This dish is among the best of the Norwegian delicacies.

Jellied Veal

1 quart cold water
1 pound veal neck
1 veal knuckle bone
¼ cup diced celery
½ teaspoon sea salt
¼ teaspoon pepper
4 whole cloves
4 whole allspice
1 bay leaf
2 teaspoons vinegar
1 tablespoon unflavored gelatin

Put the cold water, meat, celery and spices in a large pot and bring the water to a boil. Skim off foam from the top. Cover and simmer for about 2 hours. When the meat is tender, remove and cut into tiny squares. Strain the stock and cook down the liquid to about 2 cups in volume.

Add the meat and vinegar. Dissolve the gelatin in a little lukewarm water and add. Mix well and pour into a greased 1 quart mold. Chill until firm. Decorate with thin radish slices and green pepper strips to add a touch of color. Serve with mayonnaise and sour cream mixed in equal portions. This is also good with **Mustard butter.**

This is an all-purpose delight. It can be used on open-faced sandwiches, as a side dip for various meats, and is delicious with hot or cold fish. If you enjoy the piquant taste you'll think of many uses for it.

Mustard Butter

2 tablespoons prepared mustard
1 teaspoon dry mustard
¼ teaspoon white pepper
¼ cup butter
½ teaspoon lemon juice or ¼ teaspoon vinegar

Mix together into a thick paste.

Spicy Tongue

3 small veal tongues
1½ teaspoons sea salt
½ teaspoon ground pepper
½ teaspoon ground cloves
1 large or 2 small bay leaves
2 tablespoons red wine vinegar

Place the tongues in a deep pot and cover with water. Simmer very slowly for about 1 hour. Add the spices and simmer, covered, for about 2 hours more, or until tender. Remove the skins and slice thinly across the grain. Serve with some little boiled potatoes sprinkled with chopped parsley.

This is also good on open-faced sandwiches, a Danish tradition greatly enjoyed by the Norwegians as well. Top with carrot slivers and a spoonful of mayonnaise.

The potato has often been maligned as too starchy or too filling and as a consequence has suffered culinary neglect. It is a nutritious tuber with a delightful taste to complement many entrees. The Norwegians treat the potato with respect and enjoy it often, but it is usually prepared so simply as to leave one wondering why anyone would change its attractive natural goodness by exotic attempts to hide the flavor.

Plan on the equivalent of 1 medium or 4 to 5 very small new potatoes per person.

Butter-steamed Potatoes

½ cup sweet butter
1 teaspoon salt
¼ teaspoon pepper
1 tablespoon fresh dill
a bit of chopped parsley (optional)

Wash the potatoes well and peel the skins around the middle, leaving a tiny bit of peel on the ends (this is really decorative and has nothing to do with the taste or method of cooking). Melt the butter in the bottom of a Dutch oven. Add the potatoes and the seasonings. Stir until the butter coats all sides. Cover tightly. Since steam will be cooking the potatoes, the steam should be completely contained. Cook over very low heat until the potatoes are tender and the tines of a fork slip easily into the heart. Occasionally shaking the pan will insure that the potatoes do not stick. Many ranges have temperature-controlled burners. If your range is so equipped set it on 200 °F.

Cooking time will vary with the size of the potatoes. We find that a potato measuring 1 inch in diameter will cook in about 45 minutes. One with a 2-inch diameter will cook in about an hour. To serve, pour the butter remaining in the pot over the top and garnish with dill and parsley.

Vegetables naturally

Perhaps it is because vegetables are not available in abundance throughout the year that they are enjoyed just for themselves by the Norwegians. Vegetables are rarely served with more than butter, sour cream, salt, pepper and possibly a bit of fresh dill.

The Norwegians are especially fortunate to have vast quantities of fresh spring water in which to cook such vegetables. So strong is our own feeling with regard to not cooking with tap water, strongly treated with chlorine, that we had a water purifier installed at the kitchen sink. This water is noticeably free of various contaminants and improves the flavor of many foods. Good quality bottled water is quite satisfactory.

Imaginatively prepared fresh vegetables are an excellent source of vitamins and minerals. Simple enhancements to the flavor of the vegetables lie in the subtle use of melted butter, herbs and garlic. Subtlety is the key word.

Although this Norwegian favorite seems to contradict the previous thoughts, we think it worthy of your attention.

Beets and Oranges

4 medium beets

juice of 1 orange

1 tablespoon raw sugar

sea salt and pepper to taste

2 tablespoons butter

1 tablespoon arrowroot

1 orange, sectioned

Cook the beets until just tender. Heat the orange juice in a saucepan along with the sugar, salt, pepper, butter and arrowroot flour. A bit of grated orange peel is nice too. Stir with a wire whisk and the arrowroot will blend right in. Heat until opaque and slightly thickened. Add the beets and orange sections. Mix carefully and serve.

We enjoyed this as the main course in a farmhouse just outside Askim,
Norway, where the rolling hills created a storybook setting.

Creamed
Rutabagas

2 cups rutabagas (good quality
   turnips may be substituted)

2 eggs beaten

⅓ cup cream

1 teaspoon sea salt

¼ teaspoon pepper

½ teaspoon nutmeg

1 tablespoon brown sugar

⅓ cup bread crumbs

2 tablespoons butter, melted

Peel the rutabagas or turnips. Cut into small pieces and cook in salted
water until tender, about 30 minutes. Mash with a fork and mix together with the eggs. Add other ingredients and mix well. Let stand for
about 5 minutes. Put into a buttered casserole dish and pour melted
butter over the top. Bake for 45 minutes in a preheated 325 °F. oven.
The top should be lightly browned.

Norwegian bread

Because Norway has neither the arable land nor the proper growing
season, baking wheat is not grown there. Instead, wheat for breads,
rolls, pastries and such are imported in massive quantities from the
United States and Canada. The limited amounts grown in Norway are
unsuitable for baking use for a variety of reasons. Generally the resulting flour does not rise properly. This causes a problem in the commercial baking industry, for labor laws will not allow the additional
workspan necessary for baking the slower-rising flours.

Using the quality grains from North America, Norway has developed
a devoted approach to nutritious, whole-grain breads that are really
delicious.

This is very good and may be altered to fit your diet. It can be made without
sugar or salt and with a shortening of your choice.

Whole-grain Wheat Bread

1 package yeast or 1 tablespoon
  dry yeast granules

¼ cup luke warm water

2 cups skim milk

1 tablespoon malt vinegar

¼ cup melted butter or ¼
  cup polyunsaturated vegetable oil

2 tablespoons brown sugar

1 teaspoon salt

1 cup wheat germ

4½ cups whole wheat flour

Dissolve the yeast in the lukewarm water. Heat the milk to lukewarm and add the vinegar to curdle it slightly. Then add the shortening, sugar, salt and wheat germ. Stir until thoroughly blended. Add half of the flour and beat for 1 minute. Let rest 5 minutes. Add remaining flour. Mix well and turn out onto a floured pastry cloth or breadboard. Cover and let rest 10 minutes. Knead until smooth using only enough flour to prevent the dough from sticking to your hands. Grease a large bowl and put the dough in. Turn it once so the greased side is on top.

Cover and let rise until doubled in bulk (about 1 to 2 hours). Punch down and form two oblong loaves for greased loaf pans or two rounds for baking on a cookie sheet, whichever you prefer. The taste is the same. The shape just gives your creativity a workout. Top with butter and let rise again until doubled. Bake in a 375 °F. oven 30 to 45 minutes, or until the bread shrinks away from the sides of the pan. Turn out on cooling racks and brush with butter.

Norwegian Holiday Bread
1 LARGE OR 2 SMALL LOAVES

1 package yeast or 1 tablespoon
  dry yeast granules

¼ cup lukewarm water

1 cup milk

1 cup water

½ cup butter or shortening

3 tablespoons brown sugar

1 tablespoon honey

2 teaspoons salt

3 eggs, beaten

1 cup raisins

1 cup dried currants

½ teaspoon cardamom seed

5 cups unbleached white flour

2 cups whole wheat flour

GLAZES
¼ cup milk, mixed with

¼ cup raw or confectioner's sugar

OR
¼ cup raw sugar honey
(enough to be spreadable)

In a large bowl dissolve the yeast in the lukewarm water. Heat the milk and 1 cup of water in a saucepan and dissolve the butter or shortening. Remove from the fire and add the brown sugar, honey and salt. When cooled to lukewarm add the eggs. Blend well with the milk mixture. Add to the dissolved yeast, then add the raisins, currants and cardamom seed. Sift the flours together and add the flour 1 cup at a time until all is blended in.

When you have a stiff dough, turn out on a breadboard and knead for about 10 minutes. Shape dough into a ball and put into a greased bowl. Cover and let rise until doubled in bulk. Punch down and return to breadboard to shape. Make one very large or two smaller loaves.

Since this is a holiday bread, shape into a large braid. Divide the dough into 3 equal portions (if you wish 2 braids—divide into 6 portions) and roll out into elongated rolls about 2 inches wide. Press the 3 ends together at one end then proceed to cross over and under just as you would braid a child's hair. Place on a large cookie sheet and let rise until doubled in bulk. Bake in a preheated 350°F. oven for about 30-45 minutes. Two smaller braids will naturally cook more quickly than one large braid.

While still hot from the oven spread evenly with one of the glazes.

While in Scandinavia we found an unusual sugar granule which does not dissolve during baking. Many pastries and specialty breads are sprinkled with these granules. They are tasty and unusual in appearance. You may be able to find them. If so, try brushing the tops of the braids with a bit of milk and sprinkling with this sugar. Another variation is to use colorful candied fruits or colored sugar crystals.

Waffles

Waffles are a favorite in Norway. They are usually served for dessert after the evening meal rather than at breakfast as is our custom in the United States.

Sour Cream Waffles

3 eggs, separated

1½ cups sour cream

1 cup flour

1 teaspoon baking powder

¼ cup raw sugar

¼ teaspoon sea salt

2 tablespoons melted butter

Beat the egg yolks until light and lemon colored. Add the sour cream. Sift the flour, baking powder, sugar and salt *three* times. Add the butter to the beaten egg yolks and gently stir in the flour mixture. Whip the egg whites until fluffy and fold into the batter.

If you have a Norwegian-style waffle iron, heat on the burner of the stove until a drop of water sizzles and disappears. Maintain the heat at this stage by adjusting the flame. If you are using an electric model follow directions supplied with the unit. Pour enough batter to cover only about half the iron's surface, pull down the top to closed position and cook. The batter will spread out evenly. If the waffle doesn't fill to the edges, use a bit more batter next time. If it spills out, reduce the amount of batter.

Serve with anything that pleases your group. Lingonberry jam, currant jam, sour cream or whipped cream topped with a dash of cardamom are favorites in Norway. We enjoy wild honey too.

If featured as part of a Sunday brunch, try the following special topping. It's very good and nutritious as well.

Sour Cream Butter
1 CUP

½ cup sweet butter

2 tablespoons honey

½ cup sour cream

dash of cardamom

Beat the butter until creamy. Continue beating and add the honey. Gradually add the sour cream and cardamom. Blend until fluffy.

Norwegian Pancakes

3 eggs
1 cup unbleached flour
1 teaspoon raw sugar
½ teaspoon sea salt
1¼ cups milk
1 tablespoon melted butter
confectioner's sugar (optional)

Beat the eggs until fluffy. Sift the dry ingredients and add alternately with the milk and butter. Have a griddle or large cast-iron skillet very hot. The pancakes should be very thin. If they do not spread out easily on the griddle, thin with another tablespoon of milk. As they are cooked, place in a warm oven until all are cooked, then spread with jam, honey, sour cream or **Sour cream butter** and roll up. A nice touch is to sprinkle very lightly with confectioner's sugar. Serve immediately.

Norwegians serve this to guests with coffee during the day or, topped with whipped cream, as a light dessert.

Norwegian Brown Sugar Coffee Ring

2 cups brown sugar
2 cups unbleached flour
1 teaspoon baking powder
¼ teaspoon sea salt
½ cup butter
½ cup raisins
½ cup chopped nuts
1 cup milk
1 tablespoon vinegar
½ teaspoon vanilla
½ teaspoon almond flavoring
1 egg

Mix the sugar and dry ingredients together in a bowl. Cut the butter in with a pastry blender until the butter is chopped into very small bits. Take out ½ cup of this mixture and reserve.

Add the raisins and chopped nuts. Mix the milk and vinegar together, add the flavorings, and add to the flour mixture. Beat the egg slightly and add.

Pour into a buttered ring mold and sprinkle the reserved flour-butter mixture on top. Bake in a preheated 350 °F. oven for 45 minutes. Check with a toothpick or broomstraw.

Norwegian Spice Cookies
3-4 DOZEN

⅓ cup butter

⅔ cup brown sugar

1 egg

1 cup flour, sifted 3 times before measuring

¼ teaspoon cardamom

¼ teaspoon cinnamon

¼ teaspoon ground cloves

¼ teaspoon nutmeg

¼ teaspoon salt

¼ teaspoon baking powder

¼ teaspoon pepper (yes, that's right, pepper)

⅓ cup raisins

⅓ cup chopped nuts

Cream the butter and sugar. Add the egg. Beat until fluffy. Add the flour and spices, then raisins and nuts. Drop by small spoonfuls 2 inches apart on a greased cookie sheet. Bake 10 to 12 minutes in a preheated 350 °F. oven. Serve with **Buttermilk delight.**

Buttermilk Delight

Thoroughly chill certified raw buttermilk and serve with 1 or 2 table-spoons of wild honey in chilled mugs. For an added treat, put sliced fresh peaches in the bottom of the cup. Top with a dash of cardamom. A refreshing and very nutritious drink.

Rice Pudding

1 cup brown rice

3 cups milk

2 eggs

½ cup raw sugar

¼ teaspoon sea salt

1 teaspoon vanilla

2 tablespoons butter
½ cup raisins
2 sticks whole cinnamon

Cook the rice as usual for 20 minutes. Rinse in cold water and drain. Bring the milk to a boil and remove from heat, then let stand until a skin forms on top. Lift the skin off with a fork and let the milk cool slightly. Beat eggs with a fork and add, stirring to blend. Add the remaining ingredients except for the cinnamon sticks. Pour into a baking dish and poke in the cinnamon sticks. Bake in a preheated 350°F. oven 30 or 40 minutes, or until firm. Remove cinnamon and serve warm from the oven with thick cream or sour cream.

Use any fresh berry, cooked dried fruit, or combination with this.

Fruit
with
Egg Cream

1 egg
1 cup milk
1 tablespoon raw sugar
¼ teaspoon of one of the following:

    vanilla flavoring
    cinnamon
    cardamom
    nutmeg

Beat the egg vigorously. Mix the milk, sugar and flavoring and bring to a boil. Add a little of the hot milk to the beaten egg and stir. Stir the egg-milk mixture into the rest of the milk and cook until it is thickened and quite smooth. Pour this creamy sauce over individual servings of fruit.

We are quite sure that national pride is responsible for a small argument about this delightful dish. We were told by a Danish friend that it is Danish in origin. We enjoyed it in a Norwegian household where it was labeled strictly Norwegian. We are not really sure that it matters.

Cold Soufflé

1 envelope unflavored gelatin

¼ cup water

4 egg yolks

½ cup sugar

⅓ cup rum or 1 teaspoon vanilla extract or 1 teaspoon almond flavoring

1½ cups raw heavy cream, whipped

cardamom

Dissolve the gelatin in the water. In the top of a double boiler beat the egg yolks until light and fluffy. Add the sugar and gelatin. Place over the bottom half of the double boiler. Cook over medium heat, stirring constantly until the mixture thickens. Cool to room temperature (put ice in the bottom of the double boiler to speed up the cooling).

When cool, add the flavoring and fold in the whipped cream. Refrigerate in individual molds or one large one. Serve with a spoonful of additional whipped cream and a dash of cardamom.

"The proof of the pudding . . .

. . . is in the eating." We hope you'll try any or all of these Norwegian recipes. They were selected from our experience to satisfy the taste buds and efforts toward good nutrition . . . naturally!

Sweden   Dominating the center of Scandinavia, Sweden is a vast land of lakes, mountains and forests. Like its neighbors, Sweden is exposed to the warm Baltic with its vast stores of herring. Thousands of fresh-water lakes produce tons of delicious fish, including some of the most delightful salmon to be found anywhere.

This proximity to great stores of fish together with a viable agriculture and a traditional love of good food, helps to insure a consistent supply of nutritionally-correct foodstuffs. Sweden's people eat well —not just abundantly but nutritionally. Swedish housewives are discriminating in what they feed their families, and most have an inherent regard for the quality and nutritional value of food. They are as health-minded as any people we have observed, insisting on good nutrition and daily exercise. These hardy offspring of the Vikings thrive on physical activity and have an almost reverent love of the out-of-doors. They ride bicycles, hike in the mountains, walk in the woods, enjoy calisthenics, athletic sports, swimming and boating.

Although we occasionally detect a bit of French, Danish and German influences in their cuisine, items of the Swedish table such as *Gravad Lax, Kaldomar, Jansson's Temptation* and *Wasa Bread* are distinctly Swedish in every way.

Once you've enjoyed the fine foods of Sweden, either in a restaurant, private home or from your own kitchen, you will forever be entranced by the wholesome goodness and delectable flavor of the bill-of-fare that has made the Swedish people one of the healthiest peoples of the world. So, prepare yourself for a gastronomic journey of true delight, as we look at the good foods of Sweden.

The smorgasbord

Tore Wretman, one of Sweden's finest restaurateurs and royal caterer to Gustav VI, former reigning monarch of Sweden, declares that the "something to begin with" tables of no other country equal the *smorgasbord*. We have discussed the foods of Sweden with Mr. Wretman at length, dined at his famous Operakällaren restaurant in Stockholm, and studiously sought to prepare some of his favorite recipes in our own kitchen.

Today the *smorgasbord* is somewhat of a contradiction of the "something to begin with" tradition in the sense that it is now served as several, orderly courses that make up the entire meal. It differs from the American buffet in the numbers of dishes and the types of foods. While the *smorgasbord* of the better Swedish restaurants may feature upwards of a hundred dishes, it may indeed be kept as simple or as elaborate as you wish.

The *smorgasbord* we first encountered was, in our opinion, the most authentic to be found in all of Sweden. As we entered the main dining room at Ulriksdals Wardhus, north of Stockholm, we were immediately impressed by the quiet atmosphere punctuated by bits of low conversation and the soft clinking of chinaware and crystal.

Had the setting been anywhere else in the world, chances are there would have been heard the strains of a violin, accordion or similar music. Not so here. The presumption here is that good food, of an elaborate table, blended with light conversation, constitutes the perfect setting for dining pleasure.

As surreptitiously as possible, I stepped off the length of the table. Almost ten strides at almost three feet each calculates to be a bit less than thirty feet! That's quite a *smorgasbord!* At an average of two dishes per foot another quick calculation revealed more than sixty colorful, tasty, individual dishes. To astonish us further, many of the dishes were replaced with different entrees during the dining period.

We promptly decided that this *smorgasbord* was either the ultimate test of gastronomic stamina, or perhaps the finest opportunity to discover the largest number of Sweden's traditional foods. It proved to be both.

The *smorgasbord* is actually divided into three portions. The first offers the opportunity to try herring. (Mr. Wretman states: "A *smorgasbord* without herring is unthinkable.") Without question, Baltic herring is the finest in the world. Although it is not generally available here in the United States, occasionally it may be found, packed in tins or salt or brine. Nova Scotia herring is more readily available and is quite good, although not as sweet and tasty as the Baltic varieties of herring.

Salt Herring

If you are not accustomed to serve herring, there are a few tips that will inspire you.

If you buy salt herring get it far enough in advance of your *smorgasbord* to soak it overnight in cold water with 2 tablespoons of skim milk added. This will remove some of the excess saltiness. Clean the fish by removing heads, tails, and fins. Remove the backbone carefully and as many of the small bones as possible. Arrange the filets on a long ceramic dish. With a very sharp knife, cut the filets crosswise into thin slices. Restore the general shape of the fish by pushing the thin slices as close together as possible. Garnish with thinly sliced onion rings and tiny sprigs of fresh dill. Dill, incidentally, is the national herb of Sweden, and although it is used throughout the world and especially in Scandinavia, its use in Sweden staggers the imagination.

This is known in Sweden as Glassblower's herring and is very popular.

Spicy Pickled Herring

1 pound salt herring

1 medium red onion

¼ white or brown onion

1 small carrot

1-inch piece fresh horseradish

½ cup water

1 cup white vinegar

¼ cup raw sugar

8 whole allspice

4 whole peppercorns

¼ teaspoon dry mustard

1 bay leaf

¼ teaspoon dill seed

¼ teaspoon ground ginger

dill sprigs

Have a wide-mouth glass jar or ceramic crock handy. Soak the herring as directed above (the longer it is soaked, the less salty the taste).

Clean and debone the herring and cut into 1-inch pieces. Thinly slice the onion, carrot and horseradish. Cook the water, vinegar, sugar and spices in a saucepan until the sugar is dissolved and begins to bubble slightly. Remove from the fire and cool. Pour over the herring in the jar, spices and all. Top with the dill sprigs, cover, and refrigerate overnight before serving.

You may prepare 2 days ahead. It will keep very well in the refrigerator, but after 3 or 4 days the herring will develop a very strong vinegary flavor.

This is extremely easy, quick, and satisfying. It is one of the most authentic of the Swedish herring dishes, and is usually accompanied at the smorgasbord *by boiled potatoes.*

Herring with Sour Cream

several small herring
1 cup sour cream
½ teaspoon dry mustard
½ tablespoon raw sugar
dill sprigs

Soak the salt herring overnight in the refrigerator as directed. Rinse and pat dry. Remove skin, head, tail and backbone. Cut the filets into 2-inch pieces and arrange on a platter. Mix the sour cream, mustard, and sugar. Spread over the herring. Garnish with dill sprigs.

The simplest smorgasbord

Not every *smorgasbord* features an elaborate table with dozens to hundreds of separate dishes. Many Swedish households will present a simple *bord* of bread with butter, herring and cheese (*smor, ost och sill*). Usually the light cheeses are served here. The heavier pungent cheeses are served with dessert. Often a cheese spread will be served at the simple *smorgasbord*.

Cheese Spread

1 cup sour cream
1 cup grated Cheddar cheese
¼ cup crumbled blue cheese
¼ teaspoon sea salt
1 teaspoon caraway seed
¼ teaspoon dry mustard

Blend all the ingredients thoroughly and put into a small rounded bowl that has been lightly greased with polyunsaturated salad oil. Refrigerate overnight. Unmold to serve with individual wooden spreaders. These spreaders are traditional in Sweden, and many specialty shops featuring Scandinavian utensils have them. This spread is delicious on any thinly-sliced bread or crisp crackers.

This is a great way to use bits of leftover cheese of any variety. It is so unusual, delicious and highly nutritious that we often make up about a dozen small jars and give them at Christmastime.

Swedish Pot Cheese

2 cups leftover hard cheese (the more varieties, the better)
½ cup warm beer
¼ cup soft butter
¼ teaspoon cayenne pepper
2 tablespoons brandy (optional)

Mix all the ingredients together into a smooth, very creamy paste. Let stand for 1 hour. Mix in the brandy, if desired. Pack into small pottery or glass jars. Cover and refrigerate for 2 or 3 days, or until ready to use.

Danish variation Although the Danish section is yet to come in this book, we feel that their variation of this pot cheese is appropriately placed here.

Follow the above recipe, deleting the beer and brandy. Substitute 3 ounces vodka and 2 teaspoons caraway seed. The flavor is unusual, but delicious.

A more elaborate smorgasbord

Although an elaborate *smorgasbord* might seem to be a "cleaning out of the refrigerator" in variety of dishes, it is on the contrary a very precise assembly of carefully prepared delicacies. It may include:

> various meat cold cuts
> boiled or smoked ham
> sliced, cold roast meats (lamb, veal, pork)
>
> liver pâté
> liver loaf
> smoked salmon
> anchovies
> herring
> tuna
>
> aspics
> salads (lettuce, fruits)
> pickles
> relishes
>
> roasts
> casseroles
> chops
> steaks
> meat pies
> fowl
> cutlets
> stuffed cabbage
> vegetables in season
>
> various light desserts

beer
aquavit
buttermilk
natural juices
tea

Needless to say, main dish items can be made an integral part of the *smorgasbord* or served as entrees after the table. It is up to you.

Of all the Swedish specialties, this is probably the most famous. It is a great delicacy. In the days before refrigeration or even sophisticated preservation methods, the delicate sweet taste of fresh salmon intrigued the Swedes into finding ways to keep it available out of season. Gravad lax *was born. A deep hole was dug in the earth and lined with fresh dill. The salmon was fileted, rubbed generously with salt and sugar, then placed in the hole with dill generously layered for several feet. Dirt was replaced on top to protect against freezing. So stored, the salmon would keep reasonably well for several months and satisfy the Swede's love of salmon, hopefully until the next salmon run. Unfortunately, after some months the* gravad lax *developed a nasty strong taste as the salmon neared a rotted state. A pungent sauce was developed to mask the strange taste.*

Today gravad lax *is enjoyed under different circumstances. The process is nearly the same except for being prepared indoors in 2 or 3 days. It is still eaten with the spicy, pungent sauce. The* gravad lax *may be served as part of a* smorgasbord *or as an appetizer before a more traditional meal. It is an excellent example of the Swedish devotion to good, natural foods.*

Gravad Lax
(often appearing as *gravlax*)
SERVES 6

2 to 4 pounds cleaned and deboned salmon

3 tablespoons white peppercorns (black may be substituted)

3 tablespoons coarse salt

3 tablespoons raw sugar

1 large bunch fresh dill

Crush the peppercorns and mix with the salt and sugar. Rub the cavity of the salmon generously with this mixture. Lay one half of the salmon, skin side down, into a pan or dish large enough to accomodate the fish. Cover the meaty side with plenty of chopped dill. Place the other half on top, skin side up. Cover with a plate. Weigh down the plate with a heavy skillet filled with additional weight (stones or bricks). Cover with plastic wrap and refrigerate for 24 to 36 hours. During this time, turn the salmon, add fresh dill and return the weights.

Just prior to serving time, remove from the refrigerator and remove all dill and spices. Slice paper thin, cutting diagonally for easier slicing, with the skin side up. Remove the skin, garnish with fresh dill and serve with individual dishes of mustard sauce (see below). The salmon is, of course, raw, but has a delicate, sweet flavor *and* is very nutritious!

Mustard Sauce

1 tablespoon mild mustard

1 tablespoon dark high-seasoned mustard

1 tablespoon raw sugar

1 tablespoon wine vinegar or white vinegar

⅛ teaspoon sea salt

¼ teaspoon white pepper

3 tablespoons polyunsaturated oil (not olive oil)

3½ teaspoons freshly chopped dill

In a small bowl mix the mustards, sugar, vinegar, salt and pepper with a wire whisk. When thoroughly blended continue beating while adding the oil in a very fine stream. If the oil is added too quickly the ingredients will not mix properly. When the sauce has reached the consistency of mayonnaise, fold in the dill. Store in the refrigerator. Stir with a wire whisk when ready to serve with the *gravad lax*.

Grilled Gravad Lax

This variation is delicious served as a main course for lunch or dinner. Instead of slicing for the smorgasbord, grill over a very hot charcoal fire for 3 minutes on each side. It should be hot and nicely browned on the outside, yet still cool on the inside. Top each serving with a pat of sweet butter, a bit of fresh dill and parsley, and serve a little mustard sauce on the side.

The **Pickled beets** *give a delightful pink color to this tasty dish. The Swedes like bright garnishes to help offset the drab winter weather.*

Herring
Salad

2 cups bite-sized pieces salt herring

4 cups diced potatoes

1 cup diced pickled beets

1 cup apple, cored, peeled, and diced

¼ cup diced dill pickle

2 tablespoons finely chopped onion

1 tablespoon pickle relish

1 teaspoon wine vinegar

sea salt and pepper to taste

½ teaspoon raw sugar

¼ cup mayonnaise

½ cup heavy cream

Mix the first 7 ingredients in a large mixing bowl. Make a dressing with the vinegar, salt, pepper, sugar and mayonnaise. Blend together thoroughly. Whip and fold in the cream. Refrigerate for several hours, or overnight before serving. Fresh or pickled, thinly-sliced cucumbers make an excellent garnish.

If you are so inclined, these pickled beets may be canned successfully.

Pickled
Beets

1 pound beets

1 cup white vinegar

3 whole cloves

1 teaspoon honey

¼ teaspoon horseradish

Cook beets in unsalted water until tender. Peel, slice, and place in a jar or dish. Cook the remaining ingredients over medium heat until the mixture begins to bubble. Pour this hot liquid over the beets, cool to room temperature and store in the refrigerator overnight. Delicious hot or cold.

This would be a very appropriate dish for a smorgasbord.

Pickled Beet and Egg Salad
SERVES 4

1 cup sliced pickled beets (see above)

1 cup diced green apples (pippin is an excellent variety)

1 cup sour cream

sea salt and pepper to taste

lettuce

1 hard-cooked egg, sliced

Gently toss the beets and apples with the sour cream, seasoned with salt and pepper. Arrange on a bed of butter lettuce or romaine and surround with slices of hard-cooked egg.

This is my own version of the traditional liver loaf.

Light Liver Pâté

1 pound chicken livers

2 tablespoons grated onion

2 anchovies

½ cup sour cream

1 teaspoon sea salt

½ teaspoon white pepper

½ cup heavy cream

Cook the chicken livers in water until tender, about 8 or 10 minutes. Drain the livers, cool and grind, using the fine blade of a good chopper, to make a smooth paste. Mix all the other ingredients except the cream. Add the liver paste and blend until smooth. Whip the cream and fold in. Line a small loaf pan with waxed paper, pour in the liver mixture and refrigerate until thoroughly chilled. Unmold and serve with Swedish wooden butter spreaders.

Cold Egg Salad
SERVES 4

4 eggs

1 cup shredded red cabbage

1 cup finely chopped apple

1 cup thinly sliced pieces cooked veal, tongue, or salmon

¼ cup mayonnaise

1 teaspoon vinegar

1 tablespoon chili sauce or catsup

Poach the eggs and chill them. Mix the cabbage, apple and meat together. Mix the mayonnaise, vinegar and chili sauce together. Toss the salad with half of the mayonnaise mixture. Arrange on a bed of lettuce with eggs on top. Ladle the remaining dressing over the top.

Eggs with . . .

1 cup sour cream
¼ cup parsley
½ teaspoon sea salt
¼ teaspoon white pepper
½ teaspoon prepared mustard
½ teaspoon white vinegar
4 hard-cooked eggs, cooled and quartered

Mix all the ingredients, except the eggs, together. Gently fold in the eggs. Serve on a bed of romaine lettuce.

Variations here are endless. Add any or a combination of the following:

    smoked herring
    pickled beets
    cucumbers
    shrimp
    asparagus
    peas

If using a combination, arrange on the platter and pour sour cream over all.

In Sweden, fresh-water mussels are added to this salad. If you can obtain them add ½ to 1 cup cooked, drained and minced mussels.

A Swedish Salad

1 cup cooked lobster pieces
1 cup cooked shrimp
½ cup sliced raw mushrooms
1 small sweet red pepper, cut in small strips
½ cup small green peas
2 cups mixed salad greens

Mix all the ingredients, except the lettuce, and chill.

Dressing	1 cup homemade mayonnaise
	1 medium tomato
	sea salt and pepper to taste
	1 tablespoon chopped parsley

In a blender puree the mayonnaise and tomato. Add the salt, pepper and parsley. When ready to serve mix with the chilled salad ingredients and serve on a bed of greens.

Herring Hash	1 filet salted herring
	2 tablespoons butter
	½ onion, thinly sliced
	2 tablespoons bread crumbs
	½ cup light cream or half and half
	½ teaspoon salt
	¼ teaspoon pepper
	½ teaspoon raw sugar
	4 boiled potatoes

Soak the herring in cold water for several hours, or overnight, to remove excess saltiness. Cut into small pieces. Melt the butter in a skillet and slowly cook the onion slices until lightly browned. Add the herring and bread crumbs. Cook until the herring is white and flaky. Add the cream and seasonings. Serve over the boiled potatoes.

This popular dish is steeped in Swedish tradition. It is served often, sometimes as a late evening supper just before the guests depart. Before the advent of the automobile, when the trip home might involve several hours on foot or horseback, such a filling supper would be welcome indeed.

Jansson's Temptation (A potato and anchovy casserole) SERVES 4	4 medium-to-large potatoes
	2 medium-to-large brown onions
	8 anchovy filets, well drained
	¼ teaspoon white pepper
	1 cup light cream
	⅓ cup bread crumbs
	2 tablespoons butter

Butter a casserole dish. Slice the potatoes, placing a layer on the bottom of the dish. Add the onions, sliced very thin, in a layer. Arrange the anchovies in a layer on top of the onions. Complete with a layer of potatoes. Sprinkle with white pepper and pour the cream over all. Top with the bread crumbs and dots of butter. Bake in a preheated 325 °F. oven until the potatoes are tender.

Having heard about Swedish meatballs all our lives, we wanted to find the most authentic recipe. Whenever we asked the question, "Who makes the best meatballs in all of Sweden?" the answer was always the same. "My mother does!" The three recipes given us were almost identical. This is the best of all three . . . naturally!

Swedish Meatballs
40 MEATBALLS

1 pound lean ground beef

¼ pound ground pork shoulder

¾ cup milk

1 teaspoon sea salt

¼ teaspoon white pepper

1 egg

¼ cup bread crumbs

2 tablespoons finely minced onion

4 tablespoons butter or polyunsaturated oil

Grind (or have ground) the meat *twice.* Mix the milk, seasonings, egg, and bread crumbs together. Let stand. Lightly brown the onion in 3 tablespoons butter. Add to the milk mixture and pour all over the meat. Knead together until smooth and thoroughly blended. Form small balls and set on a cookie sheet. Heat 1 tablespoon butter or oil in a skillet (Swedes prefer butter). Sauté the meatballs over medium heat. Move the balls around in the skillet to prevent sticking. Keep heated in the oven until ready to serve.

Meatloaf variation We enjoyed this delightful variation in the home of friends in the Bromma District of Stockholm.

Follow the directions above as for Swedish meatballs except for increasing the bread crumbs to ½ cup and adding ¼ teaspoon nutmeg. Shape the meat mixture into a loaf, place in a buttered pan and brush with egg. Sprinkle a few bread crumbs on top. Add ½ cup water in the bottom of the pan and baste while baking for 1 hour in a preheated 350 °F. oven. Remove the loaf to a platter and thicken the juices with 1 tablespoon arrowroot mixed with ½ cup cream. Stir until thick and smooth. Let each guest ladle this gravy over several thin slices of the loaf. Good boiled potatoes or noodles go well with this dish.

Salmon Custard

1 tablespoon butter

2 potatoes

½ pound smoked salmon

1 tablespoon finely chopped fresh dill

½ teaspoon white pepper

3 eggs

1½ cups milk

Butter a 10-inch round, shallow baking dish. Use leftover boiled potatoes or freshly boiled ones. Slice the potatoes into the bottom of the dish. Lay thinly sliced salmon on top. Sprinkle with the dill and pepper. Beat the eggs until frothy, add the milk and blend. Pour over the potato and salmon layers. Bake in a preheated 375 °F. oven for 30 to 45 minutes. Shake the pan and if the custard seems firm, test gently with a knife. When the knife comes out clean, the custard is ready.

Swedish Oven Lobster Omelet

2 tablespoons butter

¼ cup bread crumbs

1 cup lobster meat

4 eggs, separated

1 cup milk or light cream

½ teaspoon sea salt

Butter a baking dish. Sprinkle bread crumbs evenly over the bottom. Place the lobster meat evenly over the bread crumbs. Beat the egg yolks until fluffy. Add the milk and salt. Beat the egg whites until stiff and fold into the beaten yolks and milk. Pour over the lobster and bake in a preheated 375 °F. oven for 20 to 30 minutes, or until set.

Variation Use salmon, herring, anchovies, mushrooms, or asparagus in place of the lobster. Delete the salt if using anchovies or herring.

Sautéed	4 veal kidneys
Veal	1 tablespoon unbleached flour
Kidneys	½ teaspoon sea salt
SERVES 4	½ teaspoon pepper
	2 tablespoons butter
	2 tablespoons sherry
	chopped fresh parsley

Rinse the kidneys and remove the membrane, fat and white veins. Slice about ¼ inch thick. Dust each slice with a mixture of flour, salt and pepper. Brown quickly on both sides in butter; 3 or 4 minutes should be enough. Add the sherry just before serving. Sprinkle with some freshly chopped parsley.

Variations   Add ½ cup chopped onions, browned in the butter before cooking kidneys.

Add ½ cup sliced mushrooms with the sherry and cook until tender.

Add 1 cup beef broth and thicken with 1 tablespoon cornstarch before serving.

You may substitute lamb or pork kidneys but veal is the first choice. The younger the animal the more tender and flavorful the kidneys. If you use lamb, plan 2 per person. Soak lamb or pork kidneys in cold water for several hours before using. Pork kidneys are much stronger in flavor.

Stuffed	2 large onions, peeled
Onion	½ pound veal or ¼ pound veal and ¼ pound beef, ground twice
Leaves	1 tablespoon bread crumbs
	sea salt and white pepper to taste
	¾ cup cream
	2 tablespoons butter

Bring 1 quart of water to the boil and plunge in the onions. Cook quickly until just beginning to separate. Cook and separate the leaves. Save the small inside leaves for another use.

Mix the meat, bread crumbs, seasonings and ½ cup of the cream. Put about 1 tablespoon of the meat mixture in the center of an onion leaf and fold over to cover. When all the onion leaves are wrapped, lay them

in a buttered baking dish with the loose edges down. Dot with butter
and pour the remaining ¼ cup cream over the top. Bake in a preheated
375°F. oven for about 30 minutes. Baste several times during cooking.

Although there are no desserts included in the smorgasbord, *there are a
number of appropriate fruits to complete the table. This delightful dish is
another example of the Swedish demand for natural foods. It is as much a
fruit stew as a soup, yet neither really describes its goodness. There are
many suitable variations, so let your own tastes be the judge of which to
use.*

Fruit Soup

1½ quarts water (more if needed)

½ cup pitted dried prunes

½ cup dried apricots

½ cup dried peaches

½ cup raisins

½ cup tart apple slices

1 stick cinnamon

1 tablespoon lemon juice

1 teaspoon grated lemon rind

3 tablespoons quick tapioca

½ cup natural honey or ½ cup raw sugar

Bring the water to a boil in a large kettle (the fruit volume will increase). Put in the prunes, apricots, peaches and raisins. Turn off the
fire, cover, and let soak for 1 hour. If you prefer, soak fruit overnight in
cold water. Cook with the apple, cinnamon stick, lemon juice, rind,
tapioca and honey until thick and clear, stirring often with a wooden
spoon to prevent sticking. If not sweet enough, add more honey. Cool
and serve in clear glass dishes or parfait glasses.

   An interesting variation is to reduce the water to 5 cups and add 1 cup
organic berry juice (grape, raspberry, boysenberry, blackberry or
strawberry). Arrowroot flour may be substituted for the tapioca (use a
scant 2 tablespoons).

   For a creamier soup force the fruit through a sieve or put in the
blender and puree.

There are a number of good toppings for fruit soup, such as whipped cream, a few whole berries, sour cream or ice cream. But far and away the best is the one below.

Swedish Cream

2 tablespoons butter

2 tablespoons unbleached flour

1 tablespoon raw sugar or honey

1 cup light cream

2 eggs

1 teaspoon vanilla extract

Melt the butter over low to medium heat. Add the flour and stir with a wire whisk until blended. Add the sugar and cream, stirring constantly, until mixture thickens, about 5 minutes. *Do not let boil.* Remove from fire. Beat the eggs until light and lemon colored. Pour the hot mixture into the eggs a little at a time, stirring constantly. When thoroughly blended, put back over low heat and stir for an additional 2 minutes, or until thickened. If left too long the cream will appear curdled. If so, put in the blender. Add the vanilla last. Chill and serve for each guest to use over the fruit soup. This sauce has a most delicate and pleasing taste.

Fruit Salad

The fruit salad of the smorgasbord *table at Ulriksdals Wärdhus looked so inviting, it was the first thing we wanted to try. As we started to take portions, our host leaned over and quietly whispered, "Not now . . . that is for later." At our next trip to the table, our host again whispered, "Not yet," as we reached for the fruit. Each time we made an attempt to try the fruit salad, our host led us toward another exotic dish of the true* smorgasbord *order. We never had the chance to try it.*

Several evenings later we were invited to dinner at a friend's home in Solna. The husband had been with us at Ulriksdals Wärdhus during our luncheon. At the conclusion of dinner, his wife brought out the most tempting fruit salad we had ever seen. Both looked as us, smiled and in unison said, "NOW!"

This delicious salad was topped off with an exquisite lemon sauce, made by the husband. Therefore it is called "Gunnar's Lemon Sauce."

Wash, pare, and cut into bite-sized pieces, any fruit in season: apples, oranges, grapes, firm berries, pears or grapefruit. Put pieces into a large bowl of water and ice cubes to which the juice of 1 lemon had been added. When all the fruit is prepared, let set for several minutes then drain thoroughly. This process will prevent the fruit from discoloring. Serve immediately in chilled individual compotes. Top with Gunnar's Lemon Sauce.

Gunnar's Lemon Sauce

5 egg yolks

1 cup water

¾ cup raw sugar

juice of 1 lemon

½ teaspoon finely grated lemon rind

1 cup heavy cream

Beat the egg yolks until fluffy and light. Add the water and sugar. Cook over medium heat, stirring constantly with a wooden spoon or wire whisk, until it thickens and just begins to bubble. Put the pan into ice water immediately and stir vigorously. Add the lemon juice and rind. Stir until cooled. Whip the cream until stiff and fold into the cooled egg mixture. Chill. Spoon over the fresh fruit salad.

Often there is no rational explanation for tradition. This tasty soup, which we are told is a one-dish favorite in Sweden, is usually served on Thursday night. Why it is served on Thursday night was never explained. We first tried it on a cold Saturday evening. It was just as delicious.

Pea Soup and Pork

1 cup dried yellow split peas

3 cups water

½ pound salt pork

1 large onion

2 whole cloves

1 bay leaf

⅛ teaspoon powdered marjoram

⅛ teaspoon thyme

½ teaspoon sea salt

½ teaspoon freshly ground pepper

1 teaspoon raw sugar

Soak the peas overnight in cold water. Rinse and put into a large pot with 3 cups water and the salt pork. About 2 hours before serving, add all other ingredients to the pot and simmer over a low heat for about 1½ hours. The peas should be tender but not mushy. Remove the bay leaf and cloves. Remove the pork and slice thin. Place the little pork slices into individual bowls and fill with the soup. Good bread, butter, a small salad and a light dessert complete the meal.

Swedish Cabbage Soup
2-DAY METHOD

2 teaspoons whole allspice
1½ quarts water
2 lamb shanks
1 beef bouillon cube
1 teaspoon sea salt
½ teaspoon pepper
1 tablespoon parsley
½ cup chopped onions or leeks
¼ cup diced parsnip or turnip
½ cup diced carrots
1 cup diced potatoes
4 cups shredded cabbage

First day   Tie the allspice in a cheesecloth bag. Put in a large pot with the water, lamb shanks, bouillon, salt, pepper and parsley. Simmer, covered, for about 3 hours. Cool and refrigerate overnight.

Second day About 1½ hours before serving, skim the fat from the top of the soup and remove the shanks and allspice bag. Cut as much meat as possible from the shanks and return to stock. Wash, peel and dice all the vegetables except the cabbage. Simmer about 30 minutes until carrots and potatoes are tender. Add the cabbage and cook, covered, until the cabbage is tender, about 30 minutes. Serve with Swedish rye bread and sweet butter.

Fish Soup á la Olde Town

1 cup white fish, in pieces
1 cup small shrimp
2 fresh tomatoes
1 tablespoon freshly chopped parsley
½ cup diced celery
½ teaspoon salt
½ teaspoon pepper
½ teaspoon saffron
1 clove garlic
1 bay leaf

Place the fish and vegetables in a pan. Add only enough water to cover. Season with salt, pepper, saffron, garlic and bay leaf. Cook slowly for 25 to 30 minutes. Remove garlic and bay leaf. Serve piping hot.

Shellfish Salad
SERVES 4

4 fresh shrimp
4 fresh scampi
4 mussels or clams
shredded lettuce
1 hard-cooked egg
8 mushrooms
1 large tomato

Cook the fish in salted water until done. Chill. Arrange a bed of lettuce on 4 individual serving plates. Slice the egg and mushrooms, quarter the tomato and distribute on each plate. Serve with **Mustard sauce dressing** (see below) or with Swedish Thousand Island dressing (equal parts of **Homemade mayonnaise** and chili sauce with a few dill seeds).

*Mustard
Sauce
Dressing*

2 tablespoons dark mustard

½ cup polyunsaturated salad oil

2 tablespoons white wine vinegar

1 teaspoon sugar

¼ teaspoon sea salt

1 teaspoon chopped fresh dill

Put all in a blender for 1 minute or beat with a wire whisk until thoroughly blended.

Several salads—one dressing

*Viking
Dressing*

½ cup salad oil

¼ cup vinegar or wine vinegar

1 teaspoon parsley flakes

1 teaspoon finely chopped chives

1 scant teaspoon chopped green olives (relish may be substituted)

1 hard-cooked egg, chopped very fine

¼ teaspoon sea salt

¼ teaspoon raw sugar

⅛ teaspoon pepper

Shake in a glass jar until thoroughly blended. This versatile dressing complements almost any salad base.

*Salad
One*

2 cups shredded cabbage

1 cup sliced beets, well drained

1 large onion, chopped

Combine all and ladle dressing over top.

*Salad
Two*

2 cups shredded cabbage

2 cups lingonberries (if available, or substitute)

Pour dressing over all.

*Salad
Three*

2 cups shredded cabbage

1 cup thinly sliced cucumbers

1 cup shredded greens

Serve with dressing.

Salad *Four*	2 large tomatoes, thinly sliced ½ cup grated horseradish

Serve with dressing.

Salad *Five*	½ cup raw cauliflower, in small pieces ½ carrot, diced ½ cup sliced cucumbers ½ cup shredded lettuce

Combine and serve with dressing.

Salad *Six*	1 cup shredded cabbage 1 cup sliced cucumbers 2 cups sliced bananas (good potassium source)

Combine and serve with dressing.

Salad *Seven*	2 cups sliced oranges or canned mandarin oranges 1 cup sliced beets, well drained 1 cup shredded lettuce

Combine and serve with dressing.

Some side dishes for fun

A part of any meal worth remembering may be inspired by a new taste sensation, something out of the ordinary or a trifle exotic in some way, a departure from the usual. There are a couple of such temptations from Sweden we'd like to share next.

French-fried Parsley

Lidingo, an island community that is attached to Stockholm by means of a single high-span bridge, is a most pleasant place. It is the former home of world famous sculptor, Carl Milles. A collection of many of his most impressive sculptures have been placed in the Italian garden near the bridge, overlooking the sea.

It was while having lunch at Forestra, within walking distance of this beautiful garden, that we encountered this delicacy. At our request, the chef gave us the recipe.

Wash and drain dry an ample quantity of fresh parsley. Separate into small sprigs. Heat polyunsaturated oil of your choice (we use peanut oil) to 400°F. Quickly drop in a few sprigs of parsley and fry for only a few seconds. They will need to be removed immediately upon cooking. Drain on to absorbent paper towels, and sprinkle with finely ground sea salt. Serve at once.

Do be careful while cooking these as the oil has a tendency to splatter more than usual. Even so, this unusual treat is worth the bother.

Anchovy Toast Treat

2 slices bread (with crusts removed)

2 tablespoons butter

1 tablespoon dark mustard

1 egg

4 anchovy filets

2 tablespoons unbleached flour

¼ cup bread crumbs

oil for deep frying

Toast the bread slices and cut in half. Mix the butter and mustard together and spread on the toast rectangles. Beat the egg. Dip the anchovy filets in the flour, egg and bread crumbs in that order. Quickly deep fry in oil. Lay the filets on toast and serve piping hot.

While you have the oil hot, fry some parsley sprigs and serve alongside—the flavors are very complementary.

Standing in the surroundings of a pleasant pear arbor in Bromma, we asked Ingrid to share her excellent recipe for Sailor's Beef. Some weeks later she sent it to us. We tried it shortly afterward in our own kitchen.

Sailor's Beef

1 pound bone-free beef (rump or similar)

2 tablespoons butter

1 teaspoon sea salt

¼ teaspoon white pepper

3 large yellow onions, sliced

10 medium potatoes

1½ tablespoons unbleached flour

½ cup water

½ cup beer or ale

Cut the meat into slices and pound with your hand. Heat a frying pan and melt the butter. Fry the beef pieces until brown on both sides over a fairly hot fire. Season with salt and pepper. Remove the meat and fry the onions in the same pan. Set aside.

Peel and slice the potatoes. Put layers of potatoes, onions and beef into an oven-proof casserole. Add the flour to the remaining butter-beef juices and make a gravy, gradually adding and stirring in the water-beer mixture. Pour over the beef, cover and bake in a preheated 350°F. oven for about 45 minutes, or until the potatoes and beef are tender. Serve directly from the pot. Good with Swedish rye bread and butter.

Potatoes grow in abundance in Sweden and are widely used as a food staple. The Swedes love them and they are part of almost every meal. They boil them, flake them, steam them, and always enjoy them. The following is typically Swedish.

Oven-crisp Potatoes
SERVES 4

4 medium-to-large potatoes

4 tablespoons butter

sea salt and pepper to taste

Wash, peel and slice the potatoes about ¼ inch thick. Lightly butter a large cookie sheet. Lay out the slices in a single layer. Dot each slice with a tiny bit of butter. Bake in a preheated 350°F. oven for 20 to 30 minutes. Turn once. They will become beautifully browned and quite crisp. Potatoes cooked in this manner are much healthier than those deep-fried.

The history of käldolmar *is very interesting. In the late eighteenth century, Sweden's King Charles XII led his Carolines in battle against Russia. His conquest took him as far as Turkey, where he was defeated and interned by the Turks. He later escaped and rode back to Sweden on horseback, alone. The Turkish Pasha sent his bankers to Sweden in an attempt to negotiate certain war reparations. They remained for several years. While they were there they had Swedish cooks prepare their favorite food,* dolmar, *which is Turkish for a dish containing meat, raisins and rice wrapped in grape leaves, then baked and covered with an egg sauce. Since there were no grape leaves in Sweden, cabbage and onion leaves were substituted. The Swedish word for cabbage is* käl, *and* lök *for onion. Thus,* lökdolmar *and* käldolmar.

In the intervening years, käldolmar *has become a national dish in Sweden.*

Käldolmar

4 tablespoons rice
4 tablespoons butter
1 cup milk
1 teaspoon sea salt
½ teaspoon white pepper
¾ pound ground beef
¾ pound ground pork
1 medium head white cabbage
2 tablespoons treacle (honey may be substituted)
¾ cup beef bouillon
1 tablespoon unbleached flour
⅓ cup cream
½ tablespoon soy sauce

Wash the rice and fry until golden brown in 1 tablespoon butter. Add the milk and cook for 20 minutes until the rice is done. Add half the salt and pepper. Put into the blender and puree for about 1 minute. You will have a porridge mixture. Let this cool while you combine the beef and pork. Blend with the porridge. Cut out the hard center of the cabbage head and discard. Boil the head until bright green in color and partially cooked. The leaves should come apart easily but should not be limp. Loosen and separate about 12 full leaves. Cut away the hard thick stem portion so they will roll easily. Divide the meat mixture as evenly as possible onto the leaves of cabbage. Fold them into little parcels. Grease a large skillet or baking dish and place the cabbage leaves folded side down. Melt the remaining 3 tablespoons butter and blend with the treacle. Add the remaining salt and pepper and the beef bouillon and pour over all. Cover and bake in a preheated 300°F. oven for 1 to 1½ hours. Baste about 4 times during the cooking. They will brown to a nice color. When done, remove to a heated serving dish.

Mix the flour with the juices left in the pan and a little butter, stirring with a wire whisk. As soon as it is thoroughly blended, add the cream, then the soy sauce. When well thickened pour over the cabbage.

Swedes serve the *käldolmar* with steamed potatoes or brown rice. The nutty flavor of the rice blends well with the cabbage.

Please don't skip over this one because snow grouse may not be available! Substitute Rock Cornish game hens, available everywhere. In the preparation we use several slender poultry skewers to hold the shape.

Snow Grouse
SERVES 4

2 slices bacon

1 chicken liver or a 2-inch slice calf's liver

4 Rock Cornish game hens (or grouse), cut in half

sea salt and pepper to taste

¼ cup butter

2 cups raw cream

1 cup sour cream

1 teaspoon lemon juice

Cook the bacon, cool and crumble into very small pieces. Cook the liver, cool and chop into very small bits. Season the hen halves with salt and pepper. In a cast-iron skillet brown the hens in butter. Pour the cream over the browned birds and let it begin to bubble. Remove from the stove, cover and cook in a very slow oven (275°F.) for 45 to 60 minutes. Check often and baste as necessary. As soon as they are tender, remove to a serving platter and keep warm while preparing the sauce. Stir the sour cream and lemon juice into the liquid remaining in the skillet.

When smooth, mix in the bacon and liver bits. Pour this sauce over the birds and serve. For a touch of Swedish authenticity serve lingonberry preserves on the side. If not available, substitute raspberry, cranberry, red currant or cloudberry* jam.

*A delicious wild berry which looks like an overgrown unripe raspberry and has a delicate aroma.

This Swedish favorite resembles hamburger patties with potatoes, beets and onion mixed into the chopped beef.

Biff à la Lindstrom

1 pound ground chuck or any lean ground beef
1 large or two small potatoes, cooked and mashed
1 small onion, chopped fine
½ cup pickled beets, drained and finely chopped
1 egg
1 tablespoon chopped capers
½ cup cream
   salt and pepper to taste
1 tablespoon sweet butter

Mix all the ingredients together except the butter, kneading with the hands. Heat a heavy skillet and melt the butter. Form the meat mixture into patties and cook until browned, about 5 minutes on each side. Serve at once.

Variation Top each patty with a fried egg.

Beef Roulades Stuffed with Onion

3 to 4 tablespoons butter
¼ cup finely chopped onion
1 pound lean beef, ground twice
1 medium potato, cooked and mashed
¼ cup bread crumbs
1 egg
¾ cup cream
1 teaspoon sea salt
½ teaspoon white pepper
1 whole onion, sliced paper thin
1 tablespoon chopped parsley

Use 1 tablespoon of the butter to sauté the chopped onions until transparent and limp. Remove to a large bowl and combine with the ground beef, mashed potatoes, bread crumbs, egg, ½ cup cream, salt and pepper. Mix together well. On a piece of waxed paper or breadboard, roll or pat out the mixture to a ¼-inch thickness. Cut into rectangles about 4 x 6 inches. Place the thinly sliced onion on the meat and gently roll up. Chill for about 1 hour. Brown in a heavy skillet with the remaining butter.

Place fried roulades on a platter and keep warm in the oven. Pour the remaining ¼ cup cream and parsley into the skillet and heat until a gravy is formed, stirring to prevent sticking. Pour over the roulades and serve.

Variation   We have used veal as substitute for the mature beef with excellent results.

Bacon, Apple, and Onion Skillet Dinner

3 tablespoons butter

1 pound Canadian bacon, sliced ⅛ to ¼ inch thick

2 large onions, thinly sliced

2 large cooking apples, sliced

¼ teaspoon sea salt

½ teaspoon brown sugar

1 whole clove

½ teaspoon freshly ground pepper

Melt the butter in a large skillet. Brown the bacon on both sides. Remove. Slightly brown the onions. Put the bacon back into the skillet. Add the apples and seasoning, except pepper. Cook, covered, over low heat until apples are tender. Check regularly and move them around in the skillet to prevent sticking. Remove the clove and grind fresh pepper over the top of all. Serve immediately.

A little about breads

Gustav Wasa, King of Sweden in the sixteenth century, was called the Rye King, for he advocated the raising of rye grain for the health of the nation. Wasa Bread, a thin, cracker-like bread, is to be found in every Swedish household today. It is generally referred to as Crisp Bread or Wasa Bread. For centuries this healthful bread was baked in the home, but inasmuch as the baking methods are extraordinarily time consuming, it is now produced primarily in one baking plant at Filipstad, some four hours from Stockholm. Today, this Swedish traditional bread is exported to more than fifty countries of the world under the trade name Ry-King. It is an excellent accompaniment to any Swedish meal.

This tasty bread is not only nutritious, but provides a food form of roughage in the diet. An excellent recipe for a similar bread is to be found in the section on Finland under **Finnish hardtack.**

This is an unusually good bread, and in our opinion, the best of the Swedish loaf breads.

Swedish Rye Loaf
2 LOAVES

1 package yeast or 1 tablespoon yeast granules
¼ cup luke warm water
1½ cups skim milk
½ cup water
2 tablespoons shortening
½ cup brown sugar
1 teaspoon sea salt
1½ teaspoons caraway seed
½ teaspoon anise
1 teaspoon orange rind (fresh or dried)
3 cups unbleached wheat flour
2 cups rye flour

In a large bowl dissolve the yeast with ¼ cup lukewarm water. Combine the milk, ½ cup water, shortening, sugar, salt and spices. Heat until shortening is melted and sugar dissolved. Cool to lukewarm and add to the yeast mixture. Sift the flours and add to the liquid a little at a time to form a stiff dough. Sprinkle a little flour on a breadboard, turn out the dough and let it rest for 10 minutes. Knead until smooth and turn into a lightly buttered bowl, turning once so that the buttered side is up. Cover and let rise until doubled in bulk. Punch down and knead well. Divide into two loaves and bake in a preheated 375°F. oven for 35 to 45 minutes. Bread will shrink slightly from the sides of the loaf pan when done. Turn out on cooling racks and brush with milk.

Breakfast in Sweden, as in almost all of Europe, consists of a simple bill of fare. A glass of vegetable or fruit juice, crisp bread, hard rolls, rye toast, perhaps a bit of jam, and coffee constitutes the entire meal.

These delicious hard-on-the-outside, soft-on-the-inside rolls will keep for several days, especially if wrapped in plastic or kraft paper.

Hard Rolls

1 package yeast or 1 tablespoon dry yeast granules

1 cup lukewarm water

2 tablespoons shortening

1 tablespoon raw sugar

1 teaspoon sea salt

3½ cups unbleached flour

2 eggs, separated

Soften the yeast in ¼ cup lukewarm water. Combine the remaining ¾ cup water with the shortening, sugar and salt. Stir until the shortening

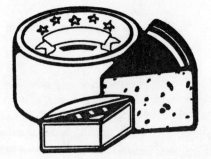

melts. Beat in 1 cup of the flour. Beat the egg whites until stiff and add. Add to the yeast blend with the remaining flour to form a stiff dough (it should be softer than bread dough). Place in a large bowl and cover. Let rise until doubled in bulk. Punch down and allow to rise again. Punch down and divide into 2″ x 3″ oblong rolls. Put into a large baking pan and brush the tops with the egg yolks mixed with a little water. Let rise again until doubled in bulk. Before putting the rolls in the oven to bake, set a large flat pan, filled ¾ full with boiling water, in the bottom of the oven. This will make the rolls crusty. Bake in a preheated 425°F. oven for about 20 minutes. Serve with plenty of good sweet butter.

Swedish Pancakes

3 eggs

1 tablespoon raw sugar

½ teaspoon sea salt

1 cup light cream

1 cup unbleached flour

¼ cup sweet butter

1 cup ice water

Beat the eggs until fluffy. Add the sugar, salt and cream. Blend until smooth. Sift the flour and add. Beat until smooth. Melt the butter and let it cool, then fold in. Fold in the ice water. If you have a divided Swedish pancake pan, use it now. If not, a heavy cast-iron skillet works well. Brush the cooking surface with a little unsalted butter. Pour the pancakes about 3 inches in diameter. If not served immediately, keep warm in the oven. Serve with fresh berries or jam between the cakes.

Fun variation   While visiting friends in the mountains, a beautiful fresh snow had fallen in the late afternoon. It was fun to scoop up the fresh snow and substitute it for the cup of ice water in this pancake recipe.

Another variation   Cook the pancakes in an 8- or 9-inch skillet, one at a time. You will need four. Stack them on a platter with berries or jam between the layers, forming a torte. Cover the stack with a thick layer of whipped cream, raw if possible, and a dash of cinnamon. They will be warm and cold at the same time.

Apple
Snow

4 tart apples

2 eggs, separated

¾ cup confectioner's sugar

1 cup cream

2 tablespoons raw sugar

¼ teaspoon cinnamon

¼ teaspoon vanilla

Wash, peel and finely grate the apples, discarding the cores. Put the apples into the small bowl of an electric mixer. Add the egg whites and confectioner's sugar. Beat for about 15 minutes. Pour into compote dishes and chill thoroughly.

Beat the egg yolks until lemon colored. Add the cream and raw sugar. Cook in the top of a double boiler until thick, stirring to prevent lumping. When quite thick remove from the fire, add the cinnamon and vanilla. Chill and serve, ladled over the apple snow.

For a healthier version substitute a variable amount of honey (to your taste) for the confectioner's sugar.

Ingrid's pear arbor in Bromma proved to be more than a beautification to their backyard. It produces an overwhelming abundance of fruit. So much in fact, she felt compelled to use them up in every conceivable way and on every possible occasion. She invented this recipe on the afternoon of our visit. Naming the dish occupied us for some time at the dinner table.

Lacy
Pears

8 fresh pears

3 tablespoons butter

½ cup brown sugar

½ cup water

1 teaspoon arrowroot

8 Swedish lace cookies

whipped cream

Wash, peel and cut the pears into halves. Scoop out the core. Butter a baking dish heavily with the butter. Lay out the pears, rounded side up in the dish. Combine the sugar, water and arrowroot. Pour over the pears. Cover and bake in a preheated 325°F. oven until tender, about 30 minutes.

At serving time, crumble about 8 **Swedish lace cookies** over the top of the pears. Top with whipped cream. Serve an additional cookie on the side of each serving dish.

Swedish Lace Cookies

½ cup dark molasses
½ cup raw sugar
½ cup butter
1 cup sifted unbleached flour
dash of sea salt
1¼ teaspoons baking powder

Combine the molasses, sugar and butter in a saucepan. Bring to a boil for a full minute, stirring constantly with a wooden spoon as this mixture will scorch or burn quite easily. Remove from the fire. Stir in the dry ingredients. Place the pan over hot water to keep the mixture soft. Drop by teaspoonsful onto a greased cookie sheet about 3 inches apart. They will spread out in cooking and become very lacy looking, hence the name. Bake in a preheated 350°F. oven for 8 to 10 minutes. Watch them very carefully. As soon as they turn a trifle dark in color, remove from the oven and let set for a few minutes. Carefully lift off with a spatula onto paper towels. They will become brittle and candy-like. Keep in an air-tight container as moisture will cause them to become limp and sticky. Needless to say, don't attempt these on an extremely humid day.

A good variation Shape into cones while still hot (setting into a liqueur glass will help set the shape). Fill with unsweetened whipped cream.

Swedish Cones
4 LARGE OR
8 SMALL CONES

1 egg, separated
¼ cup raw sugar
dash of sea salt
½ teaspoon vanilla
1½ tablespoons melted butter
2 tablespoons unbleached flour

Beat the egg yolk until fluffy. Add the sugar, salt and vanilla, blending thoroughly. Add the melted butter and blend in. Sift the flour and add. Beat the egg white until stiff and fold in. The batter will be somewhat stiff before adding the egg white. Grease a large cookie sheet and dust with flour, tapping off the excess. Drop the batter by the spoonful in either 4 or 8 places with space between. Spread each into a circle with the back of a spoon (about 3-inch circles for the small cones, 5 to 6 inches for the larger ones). Bake in a preheated 400°F. oven for about 5 minutes. They should be golden but not browned. Fold two sides together and insert into a liqueur glass to hold the shape.

When they are cooled, fill with whipped cream, slightly sweetened with natural honey and a subtle hint of almond flavoring. In Sweden, berries are often used in place of the whipped cream. It's a very colorful adaptation.

On a somber dark blustery fall day, we were invited to the Bengtson home in Bergshamra for coffee. The house is located on a point of land jutting out into Brunnsviken, a large lake on the outskirts of Stockholm.

As we entered the warmth of the living room, we saw a table in the center, fairly groaning with an array of Swedish cakes, cookies, and china. This authentic Swedish torte was in the center of the table.

Lily's Cake and a Bit of Nostalgia

1 cup slivered almonds

6 egg whites

½ teaspoon baking powder

¼ teaspoon sea salt

1 teaspoon vanilla

1 teaspoon vinegar

1 tablespoon water

1½ cups raw sugar

1 cup heavy cream

2 ounces German sweet chocolate or carob bits

Toast the almonds and set aside to cool.

In a mixer beat the egg whites, baking powder, salt, vanilla, vinegar and water together until stiff peaks are formed. Begin to add the sugar a little at a time and continue beating until all sugar is added. Fold in the toasted almonds.

Line two cookie sheets with brown paper. Draw a circle about 8 inches in diameter on the paper. Spoon the meringue evenly in the center (make three or four mounds) and spread out to the edges of each circle. Bake in a preheated 225°F. oven for about 45 minutes. If the meringue should begin to turn brown, turn the oven down to 200°F. Let the layers cool on the paper, then very carefully loosen with a spatula and remove. Just before serving, whip the cream. Spread the cream between the layers and on top. Grate the chocolate on each layer and on top. Chill slightly in the refrigerator before serving. Cut as you would a cake.

Denmark
Denmark is one of the tidiest countries of Europe. Everything is bright and shining, the people genial and gay, and the food delicious and plentiful.

The smallest of the Scandinavian countries, Denmark occupies the Jutland Peninsula, extending northward from Germany into the North Sea between Norway and Sweden, and including a group of contiguous islands. The population of this small country (about half the size of Maine) is nearing five million.

Because of its geographical location, Denmark shares traditions with both Germany and the countries of Scandinavia. Its customs and foods are a curious mixture of both influences, including various subtle French intrusions on its cuisine.

The Danes are proud, happy and hard-working people.

Their agriculture is among the world's most respected. They currently produce three times their own requirements for food. Food exports of unique quality find their way to more than 140 other countries of the world.

Inasmuch as Denmark has little in the way of natural resources, they use what they have with expertise. The sea, the land and the climate are in their favor for agriculture. Winters are mild with the temperatures rarely dropping below freezing. The summers are comfortable at a consistent 68 degrees.

Denmark has an uncomplicated flat topography. In spite of this, there is much pastoral beauty. Groves of beech trees set in contrast to the pine forests and meadows are spectacularly beautiful. Adding to the scene are the trim neat farms, where the healthy foods of Denmark are produced.

Farmers there are required to serve apprenticeships in formal agricultural training, including veterinary medicine (about the same

time spent in the United States earning a Bachelor of Arts degree).
Traditional respect for food quality, intensive technical training, and
monetary incentive combine to produce Denmark's healthy foods.

Direct beneficiaries of this agricultural excellence are the Danish
housewives who have an abundance of food variety and assured,
natural quality from which to choose. Avoidance of chemical contaminants is so closely monitored, that natural quality is soon taken for
granted, and justly so.

Agricultural output for consumption at home and for marketing
abroad is handled through the sophisticated techniques of the Danish
Food Marketing Board. Acting in the spirit of cooperative action,
Danish foods bring the highest possible prices. This incentive has done
much for the sustained quality of food.

The pleasure senses have not been ignored in behalf of natural quality. Indeed, Danish cuisine is extraordinarily palate-tantalizing, as you
will see.

As is the case with the Finnish *voileipäpöytä*, Swedish *smorgasbord*
and Norwegian *køltbørd*, Denmark proudly exhibits its *smørrebrød*, the
"something to begin with," now famous the world over.

Smørrebrød (open-faced sandwiches)

Smørrebrød literally means "buttered bread," but in fact is any appropriate combination of bread, butter, and one, two or more toppings
such as shellfish, fish, meats, pâtés, sausages, eggs, cheeses, vegetables
and herbs. Like the Swedish *smorgasbord*, it can be simply presented or
elaborately served as a meal in itself.

Smørrebrød's history dates back hundreds of years to the time when
slices of bread were used as plates. Over the years the Danes, with skill
and imagination, have developed such a variety of these open-faced
sandwiches that this national dish has become an international
favorite.

One of the finest features of the *smørrebrød* is the advantage of using
almost anything you have on hand and doing it yourself. You can
quickly prepare an original party buffet, a nutritious mid-afternoon
snack, a tasty luncheon or a fancy dinner. Best of all, *smørrebrød* is

heaven-sent on the occasion of unexpected guests.

In Denmark *smørrebrød* preparation is a specialty of each household or restaurant. Many of these sandwiches are based on tradition and have never been put to paper, but handed down verbally. The true art of *smørrebrød* lies in blending all ingredients into a harmony of taste, pleasure to the eye and good nutritional value. This requires five essential things:

1. Imagination
2. A sensitive palate
3. Choice ingredients
4. A sense of symmetry and beauty
5. Loving care

The basics

Bread   Use any good, wholesome variety with body and texture, especially one with cracked or whole-grain content. Good home-baked breads are best, but health food stores and certain bakeries offer excellent varieties. Whole-grained wheat, rye, pumpernickel and high-gluten white breads are excellent for *smørrebrød*. Scandinavian rye crackers and crisp bread may also be used. Whichever bread you select should be very thinly sliced as it primarily serves as a base for a sandwich. For health reasons it is best to keep the bread intake low.

Butter   Butter for the *smørrebrød* should always be just spreadable, neither very soft nor too cold to spread easily. It is used not only for flavor and nutrition but also to provide a moisture barrier between the bread and the topping ingredients. Making your own butter can be fun. (See **Butter: blender.**)

Raw butter from a certified dairy is terrific.

Sweet cream butter has an exceptional flavor and nutrition.

Unsalted butter does not compete with the toppings.

Scorched butter can be a really unusual variation.

Garlic butter for grilled meats: Add a pinch of crushed garlic, a little lemon juice, and salt and pepper to taste. Blend well.

Horseradish butter adds a zing and a zest to beef, fried liver, and fish. Mix in a little grated horseradish, mild or strong, to your own taste.

Parsley butter is good for chopped meats and fish. Mix a bit of freshly chopped parsley, salt, and cayenne pepper with unsalted butter.

Orange butter is excellent with wild game. Blend a small amount of juice and grated rind with unsalted butter.

Curry butter is an extra treat with pork or lamb. Mix a dash of curry powder, ginger, and cayenne pepper with sweet butter.

Cheese butter: Mix in a bit of blue cheese with unsalted butter. Blend thoroughly.

Mustard butter: Mix half butter and half dark mustard. This is particularly good when well-chilled and used with cold sliced beef or ham.

Kids' butter: Half butter, half peanut butter.

Certainly this is not the entire list. You be the judge of what will work well.

Topping ingredients   (In all cases spread the butter on the bread first. It prevents drying out during preparation.)

1. Spread the bread of your choice with the butter of your choice. Add 1 or 2 very thin slices of Danish ham, cut the size of the bread. Top with a tablespoon of well-drained vegetable salad. Decorate with a very thin slice of tomato and unpeeled cucumber. Add a small sprig of watercress or parsley.

2. Top with a spoon of chicken salad. Decorate with a slice of raw mushroom and watercress.

3. **Sherry herring** atop crisp toast. Garnish with a very thin slice of lemon.

4. Thin slice of freshly fried filet of sole. Garnish with a thin lemon slice.

5. Thick layer of caviar, with twisted thin-sliced lemon.

6. Buttered rye bread with a thick slice of liver pâté. Top with a square of meat jelly and thinly sliced pickled cucumber.

7. Thin slice of smoked salmon. Garnish with Danish caviar.

8. Thin slice of salmon. Garnish with cooked asparagus tips and lettuce.

9. Top with cooked baby shrimp. Garnish with a bit of mayonnaise and parsley.

10. Butter a slice of brown bread, topped with raw ground beef. Garnish with 1 or 2 red onion rings. Put a raw egg into the onion ring with capers.

11. Top with Havarti cheese. Garnish with a dab of black currant jam.

12. Top with Samso cheese and thinly sliced cucumber garnish.

13. Top with a thick slice of Havarti cheese, lettuce and radish slice.

14. Top with bits of Danish blue cheese. Garnish with lettuce and grapes.

15. Veterinarian's Night Snack—One of the best known and most often requested. A slice of liver pâté, a slice of meat jelly and a thin slice of salted veal.* Garnish with white onion rings and fresh watercress. Pastrami or corned-beef may be substituted for salted veal.

16. Top with liver pâté and crisp bacon. Sauté mushroom slices in butter until tender then heap generously on top.

17. Top with thinly-sliced meat jelly. Roll a thin slice of pastrami into a cornet shape and insert one end through a white onion ring.

18. Top buttered brown bread with sliced roast pork. Garnish with a pitted prune, a thin apple slice and finely chopped red cabbage.

19. Top buttered pumpernickel with thin slices of beef brisket (boiled until tender and sliced across the grain. Top with chopped pickle, grated horseradish, watercress and a thin slice of tomato cut half way through and slightly twisted so it will stand.

20. Top dark bread with thin slices of **Underdone roast beef.** Top with **Homemade mayonnaise** mixed with piccalilli.** Thinly slice raw onion, season with a little salt and sugar to make crisp, and brown in very hot butter. Lay on top in a mound.

21. "Smiling Toast" is a particular favorite of the young. Toast the bread and butter. Top with cod roe and a bit of caviar. Make a cavity in the top, circle with an onion ring and place a raw egg in the center, garnished with a bit of watercress. Omit the egg for those who don't care for it.

22. For the adventuresome. Thinly sliced smoked eel topped with scrambled eggs. Garnish with freshly chopped chives. This is a typical Danish specialty.

23. Top with cooked chicken (white or dark meat). Garnish with a spiced cucumber slice and a dab of red currant jelly.

24. Top with a thick slice of Danish ham. Fry an egg in sweet butter until the white is set. Do not turn. While still sizzling, place on the ham and garnish with a thin slice of tomato and watercress.

25. Butter dark bread with scorched butter. Top with thin slices of roasted game bird (grouse or quail), sprinkle blue cheese over the top and place a small bit of berry jam in the center. Garnish with pine needles.

*Salted Veal: Begin with a loin of veal. Rub it well with coarse salt. Keep in the refrigerator for 3 days. Scrape off the salt and put into a pot with enough water to cover. Simmer for about 1 hour until tender. Put the meat into a jar and pour the juices from the pot into the jar. Seal and keep in the refrigerator. The juices will act as a pickling brine.

**Piccalilli is a spiced relish of East Indian origin. If you can't find it, make your own. Chop fine green pepper, onions, cucumber and green tomatoes. Marinate in vinegar, salt and a pinch of raw sugar.

We've given you the top 25 open-faced sandwiches on the list of Danish favorites for *smørrebrød.* There are about 200 recognized types in Denmark. Variations of your own are a must; after all, you know the tastes of your family and friends. As you develop these variations, jot them down. Eventually your personal file will resemble the bill-of-fare of the typical Danish kitchen. Remember that fresh ingredients are the constant ally of the *smørrebrød*.

Whether you serve the *smørrebrød* as the "something to begin with" part of a regular meal, as the entire meal, or as an afternoon or late evening snack, you will draw compliments and at the same time will be able to serve confidently a fare of good nutrition. Perhaps your guests will respond in Danish, *"Tak for mad"* (Thanks for the food).

One of the most memorable occasions of our lives occurred in Copenhagen when we visited Tivoli Gardens, the high point of any sojourn in that city. After touring the grounds in the company of J. Olsen, manager of Restaurant Taverna located in the Concert hall there, we returned for the evening performance of the circus. The circus has always excited us, so much so that we could scarcely think of eating. Realizing that the evening would be spent watching a menagerie of animals, high-wire performers and a raucous group of clowns, we did consent to have a bowl of soup at the Wivex restaurant around the corner. It is a charming and busy place. It was here that we discovered this marvelous soup.

Happiness with Shrimp and Corn Soup

4 cups milk

2 tablespoons butter

½ teaspoon sea salt

¼ teaspoon white pepper

¼ teaspoon paprika

1 tablespoon finely chopped onion

1 cup fresh or canned corn

1 cup very tiny shrimp

2 tablespoons unbleached flour

1 teaspoon chopped fresh parsley

Heat the milk, butter, salt, pepper, paprika and onion. If you use fresh corn, cut from the ear and add now. If canned, add later with the shrimp. Heat until butter is melted. Add corn and shrimp. Put some of the hot milk into a cup and let it cool a bit then add the flour, mixing well. Gradually add to the pan of hot soup to thicken. When thoroughly heated and thickened, ladle into bowls. Top with a pat of sweet butter and a bit of parsley.

The flavor is almost the same as celery, and since chervil is almost impossible to find nowadays, we have substituted the celery. If you want chervil, you will probably have to grow it yourself. We haven't changed the name to celery soup, because it is quite different from most soups of that name.

Chervil Soup

4 small carrots

4 stalks celery with leaves

4 cups beef bouillon

2 tablespoons butter

4 tablespoons whole-wheat flour

2 hard-cooked eggs, sliced

8 small meatballs

sea salt and pepper to taste

chopped parsley

Clean the carrots and celery, reserving the celery leaves. Boil the whole vegetables in the bouillon. When tender, remove and slice. Cream the butter and flour together. Add a little of the bouillon and blend. Add this to the pot of bouillon and blend until thickened. Remove from heat and serve in individual soup bowls. Add the celery, carrots, hard-cooked egg slices and meatballs, divided evenly between the bowls. Salt and pepper lightly on top along with finely chopped celery leaves and parsley.

This icy cold soup is perfect for luncheon on a hot summer's day. We usually get our buttermilk from a certified raw milk dairy.

Cold Buttermilk Soup

2 egg yolks

⅓ cup raw sugar

1 tablespoon lemon juice

4 cups very fresh buttermilk

1 cup heavy cream, whipped

Beat the egg yolks until fluffy. Add the sugar and continue beating until almost white. Add the lemon juice and blend. Gradually stir in the cold buttermilk. The soup should be served very cold with a large scoop of whipped cream in the middle.

Variation   A truly Danish variation is to serve with split blanched almonds and strawberry jam as a dessert.

Salads

Cucumber Salad
SERVES 4

1 large or 2 small cucumbers
¼ cup water
½ cup vinegar
¼ teaspoon salt
¼ teaspoon pepper
2 tablespoons raw sugar (we often substitute honey for sugar but not here)

Rinse the cucumber and cut or shred into thin slices (in Denmark the skin is never removed). Bring to a boil all ingredients but the cucumber. Cool. Arrange the cucumber in a dish and pour the pickling-brine over them. There should be sufficient liquid to cover completely. Cover and let stand for about 4 hours. Serve as is or on lettuce or sliced tomatoes. One slice is excellent on almost any open-faced sandwich.

Vegetable and Mayonnaise Salad
SERVES 4

2 carrots, cooked and diced
8 asparagus spears, cooked and finely cut
1 cup small green peas, cooked until just tender
¾ cup mayonnaise*

Cool the cooked vegetables. Blend in the mayonnaise and serve chilled or at room temperature on romaine or butter lettuce. Also good for smørrebrød.

*If you are using **Homemade mayonnaise**, add ¼ teaspoon tarragon vinegar before stirring in the vegetables.

Chicken Salad

¼ teaspoon curry powder
1 teaspoon Worcestershire sauce
1 teaspoon lemon juice
   salt and pepper to taste
¼ cup heavy cream
¾ cup mayonnaise
1 cup small pieces cooked chicken
1 cup tiny green peas, cooked and chilled
1 cup raw asparagus or raw mushroom slices

Add seasonings and cream to the mayonnaise. Fold in the chicken and vegetables. Serve on a lettuce leaf   tomato and watercress.

Danish
Potato
Salad

4 medium potatoes, boiled, peeled and sliced
1 cup Pickled beets, drained and sliced
1 small can sardines, drained and chopped
1 apple, chopped
1 tablespoon chopped onion
1 cup Homemade mayonnaise
2 tablespoons beet juice

Mix first 5 ingredients and then combine mayonnaise with the beet juice and fold in. Adding hard-cooked eggs, pickles and olives makes an interesting variation.

Red
Cabbage
Salad

1 cup water
¼ cup lemon juice or vinegar
2 tablespoons honey
½ teaspoon salt
1 small onion, grated
4 cups shredded red cabbage
½ cup chopped apple (optional)

Bring the water, lemon juice, honey and salt to the boil. Add the onion and cabbage. Simmer slowly, covered, until cabbage is tender, about 30 minutes. Serve either hot or cold. If served cold, add ½ cup chopped apple.

Cheeses

Samso is a beautiful Danish island in the Kattegat Sea. Samso cheese gets its name from this pleasant isle. The mild and mellow taste of this firm yet supple cheese of high butterfat content, has made it famous the world over. Both the island and the cheese are first-rate attractions.

White
Cheese
Balls

2 egg whites
1 cup grated Samso cheese
   safflower oil

Beat the egg whites until stiff. Grate the cheese and fold into the egg whites. The mixture should be thick enough to roll into balls about the size of a walnut and hold its shape. If not, add more cheese. Deep fry the cheese balls in hot oil (375° to 400°) until golden. Place on absorbent towels. Serve while still warm.

These may be made well ahead of time.

Heartier Cheese Balls

1 cup water
½ cup butter
1 cup unbleached flour
3 eggs
1 cup grated Samso cheese
½ teaspoon sea salt

Bring the water and butter to a boil in a saucepan. Remove from the heat and add the flour. Blend, cover and let stand for 5 minutes. Beat the eggs and fold into the flour mixture, one at a time. Add ½ cup of the cheese and salt mixed together. Form balls and cook in hot oil (375° to 400°) for 3 or 4 minutes until golden brown. Drain on absorbent paper. Keep warm until ready to serve, then sprinkle the remaining ½ cup cheese on top, and accompany with sliced celery and radishes as a luncheon salad.

Cheese Bars

¾ cup butter
1 cup unbleached flour
1¼ cups grated Samso cheese
½ teaspoon sea salt

Crumble the butter into the flour. Add other ingredients and knead the dough until it holds together well. Cover and let rest for 30 minutes.

Roll dough out to ¼-inch thickness and cut into oblong bars 1 inch x 2 inches. Bake at 400°F. until light brown, about 8 to 10 minutes.

Camembert Lover's Delight

4 fresh Camembert wedges
2 egg whites, stiffly beaten
½ cup bread crumbs

Dip the cheese wedges into the egg whites then into the bread crumbs. Fry in hot polyunsaturated oil turning once. When golden brown drain on absorbent paper and serve with pumpernickel toast, cold butter and berry jam.

This is served directly from the frying pan so use the most attractive one you have for the preparation.

Bacon and Chives Omelet Pie

8 slices bacon
4 eggs
4 tablespoons ice water
4 tablespoons raw cream
½ cup chopped chives

Fry the bacon, remove and drain. Beat the eggs until fluffy and add the water and cream mixed together. Have the skillet hot and pour in the egg mixture. Roll the pan and lift the edges as they become firm, letting new egg liquid roll underneath. When the omelet is firm turn off the heat. Crumble the bacon and sprinkle on top along with the chives. Run under the broiler for a minute or two, long enough for the omelet to brown nicely. Serve in wedges cut like a pie with sliced tomatoes on the side.

Variation This is good with pieces of Danish ham instead of the bacon.

Sherry Herring
SERVES 4

4 pickled herring filets
1 teaspoon chopped parsley
1 tablespoon capers
1 bay leaf
2 tablespoons raw sugar
1 tablespoon boiling water
1 tablespoon vinegar
¼ cup safflower oil
½ cup sherry

Soak the herring in cold water for several hours, rinse and dry. Cut into pieces and put into a large bowl with parsley, capers and bay leaf. Dissolve the sugar in the boiling water and mix with the vinegar, oil and sherry. Pour over the filets of herring and marinate for 2 to 3 days.

Danish Liver Pâté

1 pound pork liver
½ pound pork fat
1 onion
4 anchovy filets
2 tablespoons butter
2 tablespoons flour
1 cup milk
1 egg, slightly beaten
1 teaspoon salt
1 teaspoon sugar
½ teaspoon white pepper

Put the liver, fat, onion and anchovies through a food grinder, using the fine blade. Blend the butter and flour and add the milk. Let simmer until thickened. Add the meat mixture and blend. Add the egg. Flavor with the seasonings and bake in a loaf pan, set into another pan half-filled with water, for 50 minutes in a preheated 325°F. oven. Cool and chill.

Underdone Roast Beef

If you enjoy rare roast beef, you will love this method of cooking a Danish favorite. It is exceptionally good sliced very thin for open-faced sandwiches. Select the roast of your choice—rib, eye of round or sirloin (the tenderer, the better). The truly great thing about this recipe is the fact that it works well regardless of the weight of the roast, 3, 5, 7 pounds—whatever.

Rub the meat well with garlic. Smear with butter and sprinkle generously with freshly ground pepper. Preheat the oven to 475°F. Cook the roast for 15 minutes. Open the door and reduce the heat to 375°F. Cook at the rate of 10 minutes per pound. This is very important! At the end of cooking time remove from the oven and sprinkle well with coarse salt. We crush ice cream salt with mortar and pestle to the exact coarseness we wish. Cover immediately. Leave at room temperature until cool. Refrigerate until very cold. With a very sharp knife, cut thin slices for open-faced sandwiches. The flavor is magnificent.

We sampled this type of beef in a market in Copenhagen and were so taken by the tenderness and full, natural flavor, we bought 200 grams (a little less than a half pound), a package of crisp bread, butter, and Danish Tuborg beer, then strolled along the Havnegade and sat in a small park for our lunch. The sky was blue, the air crisp, the beef delicious.

If you have eaten this dish in Denmark, don't expect to duplicate it here. Pigs in Denmark are specially bred to produce an extremely long body with an unusually long loin. The pigs even have to stretch to eat. Everything is done to elongate their bodies, producing this exceptional long section. This is not the case with American pork. If you aren't making that comparison, however, you'll find this the most delicious you have ever tasted.

The Very Famous Danish Roast Pork

4 to 5 pounds of the best quality pork loin available (with little fat)

1 cup prunes

2 medium tart apples

1 teaspoon lemon juice

sea salt and pepper

⅓ cup cream

2 tablespoons unbleached flour

1 tablespoon red currant jelly

Have your butcher cut a large pocket in the roast as for stuffed pork chops. The slit will be half way down the side and will run the length of the loin to within about an inch of each end.

Cover the prunes with cold water and bring to a boil. Cover and turn off the heat. Let stand for 30 minutes. Drain, remove pits and pat dry. Peel the apples and cut into small pieces. Sprinkle lemon juice on them to prevent discoloring and set aside. Season the inside of the pocket with salt and pepper. Pack the prunes and apples inside as uniformly as possible. Sew up the opening with strong twine or tie by wrapping twine at intervals of 1 to 2 inches.

Season the outside with salt and freshly ground pepper. In a roasting pan brown the meat on all sides in butter. Bake in a preheated oven at

325°F. for about 2 hours. Put 1½ cups of water in the pan and bake, covered, for the first hour. Remove the cover for the last hour. When done, remove to a platter and thicken the juices by adding the cream mixed with the flour and currant jelly. Stir until thickened and serve in a gravy boat. **Butter-steamed potatoes** are perfect with this roast.

Inasmuch as pork is among the best of the Danish foods, we think this recipe for pork shoulder should be included.

Roasted Pork Shoulder

sea salt and pepper
4 or 5 pound shoulder roast

Rub salt and pepper into the roast. Put into a cold oven in a roasting pan. Set the temperature to 250°F. It is important *not* to increase the temperature while cooking. Cook for 6 hours. The meat will brown very slowly.

After the first hour pour 2 cups boiling water into a pan set under the roasting pan. When done let the roast stand for 30 minutes before carving. Serve with prunes and boiled cabbage.

These pork patties are a Danish national favorite. There seem to be as many recipes as there are families. This is the best from one family.

Rissolés

1 pound pork (ground twice)
½ cup unbleached flour
½ cup bread crumbs or oatmeal (or mixed)
1 egg
1½ cups milk
½ cup chopped onion
salt and pepper to taste
butter for frying

Mix the pork with the flour, bread crumbs and oatmeal (if used). Mix the egg with the milk and stir into the meat mixture a little at a time, blending well. Add the onion, salt and pepper. Mix well. Brown butter in a heavy skillet. Form the rissolés into rounded, oblong shapes and fry over medium heat for about 2 minutes each side. Remove. Pour about a tablespoon of water into the skillet and serve the resulting liquid over the rissolés. Very good with **Creamed potatoes.**

Creamed Potatoes
SERVES 4

4 medium potatoes
4 tablespoons butter
¾ cup cream
1 teaspoon sea salt
½ teaspoon white pepper
¼ teaspoon nutmeg

Boil the potatoes until tender. Put through a sieve. Add the butter and cream. Cook over low heat until blended, smooth and thick. Add salt, pepper, and nutmeg. Beat until bubbles appear. They will be as light as a cloud.

Danish Curdled Chicken
SERVES 4

2 small chickens, cut in half
sea salt and pepper to taste
4 teaspoons butter
4 sprigs parsley
¾ cup heavy cream
livers from the chickens, cooked and finely chopped

Season the chicken halves with salt and pepper. Brown the chicken halves in a little butter in a heavy skillet or dutch oven. When browned arrange in a single layer in the skillet. Lay a sprig of parsley and a teaspoon of butter on each half. Cover tightly and cook in a preheated 325°F. oven for about 45 minutes, or until tender. Remove to a platter. Pour cream slowly into the pan juices and stir. It will curdle or separate. Add the reserved chicken livers. Blend well and pour over the chicken. Fresh rhubarb is a good accompaniment.

Carameled Potatoes

8 to 12 very small potatoes
¼ cup raw sugar or honey
¼ cup sweet butter

Boil the potatoes until tender. Peel while still hot and rinse in cold water. Cook the honey or sugar and butter in a saucepan until it begins to turn brown. Add the potatoes and cook quickly, shaking the pan to prevent scorching.

Variation   Use 12 to 24 small onions instead of the potatoes.

Rhubarb Compote

½ cup water
½ cup raw sugar
2- inch length vanilla bean or 1 teaspoon extract
1 pound fresh rhubarb
1 tablespoon cornstarch or arrowroot

Heat the water, adding the sugar and vanilla bean to form a syrup. Cut rhubarb into ½-inch pieces and cook in the syrup until tender. Thicken with the cornstarch until ready. Pour into small compote dishes and chill according to your taste.

As a dessert variation: Pour the above mixture into a baking dish which has been buttered. Add 2 cups bread crumbs and sprinkle 3 tablespoons brown sugar mixed with 3 tablespoons chopped almonds on top. Bake at 325°F. for about 25 minutes. Serve with whipped cream.

Danish Yogurt Rye Bread

1 cake fresh yeast or 1 tablespoon dry yeast granules
1 cup lukewarm water
1 cup yogurt (buttermilk may be substituted)
¼ cup butter
1 teaspoon sea salt
2½ cups rye flour
1 cup unbleached wheat flour
milk

Dissolve the yeast in the lukewarm water. Add the yogurt, butter and salt. Add the rye flour and beat until smooth. Add the wheat flour a little at a time and mix well after each addition. Knead the dough until elastic. Put into a buttered bowl and let rise for 1 hour. Punch down, knead and form 2 loaves into greased loaf pans. Let rise until doubled in bulk. Bake in a preheated 375°F. oven for 30 to 40 minutes. Bread will shrink slightly from the sides of the pan when done. Cool on racks and brush with milk while still warm.

The lightness of these delicious rolls will surprise you.

Danish Luncheon Rolls
MAKES 18-20

1 cake fresh yeast or 1 tablespoon dry yeast granules

2 teaspoons sea salt

1⅓ cups lukewarm milk

⅔ cup water

¼ cup melted butter

2½ cups rye flour

2 cups wheat flour

1 egg white

⅛ cup coarse salt

Mix the yeast, sea salt, milk, water and butter together. Stir in the rye flour and beat. Add the wheat flour a little at a time. The dough will be sticky. Carefully roll into oblong rolls about 1½ inches x 2½ inches, using a small bit of flour to prevent sticking to the hands. Place on a greased cookie sheet about 2 inches apart. Brush the tops with egg white and sprinkle coarse salt on top. Let rise until doubled in bulk. Bake in a preheated 400°F. oven for 12 to 15 minutes.

The aebleskiver *is a cross between a pancake and a doughnut, round in shape and about the size of a golf ball, perhaps a bit larger. It is a delicious Danish tradition, great for breakfast, brunch or late snack. An authentic* aebleskiver *pan should be used. However, a very small muffin tin may be substituted with reasonable success. Shop at your favorite import house for the pan.*

Hans Christian Anderson Aebleskivers

2¾ cups sifted unbleached flour

½ teaspoon sea salt

½ teaspoon cardamom

¼ teaspoon freshly grated lemon rind

2 cups milk

⅔ cup butter

1 cake fresh yeast or 1 tablespoon dry yeast granules

8 eggs, separated

1 tablespoon raw sugar

confectioner's sugar to sprinkle on top

Blend the flour and spices. Sift once. Heat the milk and butter in a saucepan until the butter is melted. Cool to lukewarm. Add the yeast. Add the egg yolks, slightly beaten. Add the flour and stir until thoroughly blended. Sprinkle the raw sugar over the top. Cover and let rise in a warm place. Whip the egg whites until stiff and fold in. Heat the *aebleskiver* pan over medium heat or to 375°F. if your range is equipped with a controlled-heat burner. Butter each hollow of the pan with unsalted butter. Fill each ¾ full. Be sure each *aebleskiver* is well browned before turning. When cooked, sprinkle confectioner's sugar on top and serve with melted butter and honey or jam.

If you don't have the *aebleskiver* pan, use muffin tins, lightly buttered and heated until very hot in a 375°F. oven. Fill to ¾ full and bake about 15 minutes.

A tip on turning the *aebleskivers:* Use a #1, 2, or 3 knitting needle. We were quite amused to see this utensil being used in a Danish pastry shop, and began using it ourselves with much better success than with other methods.

This authentic recipe for *aebleskivers* is so superior we use it over any other Americanized version.

These are a Danish favorite and are very nutritious.

Oat Cakes

¼ cup butter

2 tablespoons raw sugar

1 cup oatmeal

2 tablespoons honey

Melt the butter in a cast-iron skillet and stir in the sugar. Add the oats and stir until blended. Turn the heat to low and cover. Cook for about 10 minutes, stirring and checking often. When the oats are golden brown, remove from the fire and stir in the honey. Rinse a small muffin tin in cold water, turn upside down and tap off the excess water. Pack the cups ⅔ full and refrigerate until very cold. Remove by running a knife blade around the edges.

Variation Quite by accident I discovered this tasty variation for the children's pleasure and highly approve of it as it is very healthy while still fulfilling their desire for sweets. While making the oat cakes one afternoon, I wondered if I couldn't add the honey during the cooking rather than waiting until last. As a result the cakes became very hard, brittle and candy-like. I cut the cups into quarters and pack them into lunches, set them out for afternoon snacks and often serve them after dinner.

We were told that a Danish baker goes to school for four years to learn the art of Danish pastry making. When he takes his final exam, if his pastry doesn't have 32 separate and distinct layers he cannot get an A, indeed he might not even pass the course.

Danish pastries are very rich and there are many variations. This recipe, although not having the 32-layer complexity, is one of the best and at the same time is relatively easy to prepare.

Danish Coffee Cake

PASTRY
1 cup milk

2 tablespoons raw sugar

1 cake yeast or 1 tablespoon dry yeast granules

1 egg, slightly beaten

3 cups flour, sifted

1¼ cups butter

FILLING
¾ cup butter

½ cup broken macaroons

½ cup raw sugar

½ cup raisins

1 egg yolk, beaten

chopped almonds

Heat the milk to lukewarm, then add the sugar, yeast and egg. Put the flour into a large bowl and crumble the hard butter into this. Work with a pastry blender until you have a finely crumbled mixture. Add the liquid and beat until it is very smooth. Cover and let rise in a warm place for about 1 hour. Roll out the dough into a long oblong strip.

For the filling, crumble the butter and macaroons with the sugar and raisins along the center of the dough. Fold the two sides up and onto the center, forming a long roll. Twist into a circle and put on a greased cookie sheet. Brush the top with a bit of beaten egg yolk and sprinkle with sugar and chopped almonds. Let rise for about an hour, or until almost doubled in bulk. Bake in a preheated 400°F. oven for 25 to 30 minutes. Serve immediately if possible.

Now, let's see if we can pass the "Baker's test."

Danish
Puff
Pretzel

PASTRY
1¾ cups butter

3¾ cups unbleached flour

1 cake yeast or 1 tablespoon dry yeast granules

½ cup cold milk

2 eggs

2 tablespoons sugar

chopped almonds

FILLING
⅓ cup butter

1 cup confectioner's sugar

chopped almonds

raisins

One cup of the butter will be "rolled" into the dough. Crumble ¾ cup of the butter into the flour. Stir the yeast into the cold milk and add eggs and sugar. Beat the dough until smooth. Set into the refrigerator to chill. Now, the secret weapon! Fill a large bowl with ice water (with even a few cubes floating around). Take a cup of the butter and with your two hands, put it into the water. Work it with your hands until it becomes soft enough to roll out into a shape. As soon as you think it is ready, get the rolling pin, which has been kept in the refrigerator to keep it cold. Roll out the butter between sheets of aluminum foil into a fairly thin square. A square of about 8 inches will work well. Put into the refrigerator to re-chill.

When both the dough and the butter are very cold, roll the dough into a square of approximately 16 inches. Lay the cold butter into the center, then fold the four corners of the dough to the center. This should completely cover the butter. Roll flat to a 16 inch square again. Bring the corners to the center and roll out again to the 16 inch square. Do this three times. After the last roll-out, mix the filling ingredients together and spread from the center outward to within 2 inches of the edge. Fold over the two sides to cover the filling. Now you have a long strip. Twist the strip into the shape of a pretzel. If you want to decorate the top, brush with egg white and sprinkle with sugar and chopped almonds. Put into the refrigerator for 30 minutes. Preheat oven to 425°F. Put the cold dough into the hot oven. Bake for 20 to 25 minutes (the cooking time will depend on how thick the pretzel becomes in the shaping).

Caramel Custard

3 eggs
¼ cup raw sugar
   pinch of salt
1 cup milk
1 cup cream
1 teaspoon vanilla
⅔ cup brown sugar

Beat the eggs until fluffy. Add the sugar and salt. Blend well. Heat the milk and cream until a skin forms on top. Lift off the skin and discard. Slowly stir the milk into the egg mixture until blended. Add vanilla.

Divide the brown sugar evenly into the bottoms of 8 small custard cups or baking dishes. Pour in the custard. Place the cups into a pan of hot water and bake in a preheated 325°F. oven until the custard is firm, 30 to 45 minutes. To test, insert a knife blade into the custard. If the knife comes out clean, the custard is set. Cool. When ready to serve, invert onto a plate. The brown sugar becomes a delicious, caramel sauce.

Any berry or combination of berries may be used. Raspberries, strawberries or blackberries are beautiful in color. Here is a great combination:

Rødgrød Med Fløde
(Thickened red fruit juice with cream)

1 cup red currants
½ cup black currants
½ cup raspberries
½ cup pitted cherries
2 cups water
1 cup raw sugar
½ vanilla bean or 1 teaspoon vanilla extract
   arrowroot (3 tablespoons for each quart of liquid)

Clean and prepare the fruit. Mash with a fork until no whole berries remain. Add the water, bring to a boil and allow to stand for 20 minutes. Put this through a sieve or muslin cloth. Return to heat. Add the sugar and vanilla bean.

Bring to a boil and skim off the froth from the surface. Measure the liquid. For each quart of liquid mix 3 tablespoons arrowroot flour with a little water and add to the juices, stirring constantly. When it begins to bubble, just before boiling, remove from the heat immediately. Rinse serving bowls with water and shake out excess. Pour in the juices. Sprinkle a little raw sugar on top to prevent a crust from forming while it is cooling. Chill thoroughly and serve with cold heavy cream.

Variation Use organically-grown juices available at health food stores. Most of these are very good, nutritious and easily available on short notice.

About beverages

The Danes are famous for their beer and enjoy it often. But, as Denmark has one of the most sophisticated dairying industries in the entire world, milk is a favorite beverage too. Since milk is an international favorite and super-charged with good nutrition, we obviously endorse its use.

The following are two other beverage favorites from our friends, the Danes.

Sunshine Punch

2 quarts fresh orange juice (frozen may be substituted)
juice of 2 lemons
grated rind of 1 lemon
¾ cup raw sugar or honey
1 cup white rum
2 bottles good white wine
lots of crushed ice

Mix the juices with the grated lemon peel and sugar or honey. Stir until dissolved (the honey takes longer, but is worth it). Add the rum and wine. Pour over glasses filled with crushed ice.

Many Danish families will keep a pot of glog going on the stove throughout the holidays, adding a bit more of this and a bit more of that as it is used.

*Christmas
Glog*

1 piece fresh ginger, about 1 inch in diameter
½ cup raisins
½ cup white raisins
1 whole cinnamon stick
1 cup brown sugar
1 cup dark beer
1 quart red wine (Burgundy or claret)

Cook everything together until the aroma is quite strong and the sugar dissolved. This can be simmered for quite a long time without hurting the flavor.

And finally . . .

As we leave the cuisines of Scandinavia and the Danish Glog with its spicy aroma, we are reminded that the need to find a new route to the lands of spices led to the discovery of the New World. That is our world of today, influenced by traditions of the old and sophisticated modern technology, and in many ways threatened by ecological imbalances. Even so, the foods of the New World can be inspiring, not only for pleasure, but for health.

The New World—America

It is remarkable that the early explorers were ever able to reach the New World in their quest for shorter trade routes to the spice-producing lands of the Indies, for life at sea in the 15th century was a terrible ordeal indeed.

Living on a diet of half-rotted meat, stale bread and red wine, the men were without most of the essential vitamins and minerals now recognized as necessary to good health. Plagued by scurvy and loss of muscle tone, these early seamen aged rapidly, many dying prematurely, simply for lack of decent nutrition. Vitamin C alone would have prevented scurvy and a variety of other maladies. Even so, the New World was discovered.

So immense was this new land, its exact size was not known for several centuries. It was a unique land with a climate spectrum from barren, arctic tundra to hot, humid, tropical jungles. It had abundant water, rich soil, deep forests, minerals and an extensive wildlife population.

It was also a land that offered new freedom. Where men could work and worship as they wished, in an atmosphere of individuality unequaled in human history. And their women were with them, bearing their children, helping with the work and cooking their meals. It was an abundant land of promise, with its wild game for the table, asparagus and greens growing in the meadows, berries and fruits from vines and trees.

From then until now, the New World has been a land of unusual richness, supplying the nutritional needs of its own population and exporting tons of harvest to those countries less able to produce for themselves.

As technology grew, the waters were harnessed for irrigation and electrical energy, the minerals were refined into everything from aspirin to textiles, and agricultural expertise developed to enviable proportions.

Even with all this capability, there are those who point with alarm to a growing and widespread malnutrition within our population. In addition, additives, extractives and synthetics have depreciated our natural foods heritage. Excessive use of sugar, dangerous pesticides, herbicides, fungicides and endless varieties of hazardous chemicals have put our prospects for good nutrition in some jeopardy.

Currently sensitive to this problem, millions have reassessed what is good and conversely, what is bad with nutrition in this land of plenty. A genuine concern is developing for a renaissance of natural foods . . . the foods that are best for us all.

There is a feeling by some that natural foods, the ones that offer a unique value to our bodies, must be dull, lifeless and uninteresting. The opposite in fact true. On the ensuing pages we will offer evidence to support that fact.

Toasted Pumpkin Seeds

It might be said that toasted pumpkin seeds were literally the start of the hors d'oeuvre practice in the New World.

On Halloween we serve toasted pumpkin seeds as an hors d'oeuvre and for trick-or-treaters too. We have done this since our children were very young, having spent many hours together preparing this tasty and nutritious snack for the event. Here's how we still do it.

Carve the pumpkin into a friendly-faced jack-o'-lantern. Set aside the pumpkin meat for old-fashioned pumpkin pie. Wash the seeds carefully, removing all of the membranous, stringy part. Dry overnight. Spread the seeds out on a large cookie sheet. Dot with a small amount of butter and sprinkle with a bit of sea salt. Bake in a preheated 350°F. oven until crisp and browned. Check often to prevent burning. Stir so they will toast evenly.

One of our greatest rewards occurred one Halloween evening as we waited for the tricksters. Three small boys made their way up our driveway toward the front door. They were eager and excited and their conversation went something like this: "Hurry, they might run out!" "Run out of what?" "Didn't I tell you . . . this is where they give those neato pumpkin seeds!" "Wow, let's go!" That kind of response to something we believe to be really good for the kids is justification for the effort. Adult visitors get them with a chilled goblet of organic cranberry juice as an hors d'oeuvre before dinner.

You may already have a recipe for these, but it may just lack a subtle nuance of this carefully developed version.

Great-Aunt Adie's Nuts and Bolts

½ box Rice Chex
½ box Cheerios
½ box Corn Chex
1 box bite-sized Ralstons
½ box stick pretzels
½ pound pecan halves or peanuts or mixed nuts
½ pound butter
½ teaspoon celery salt
½ teaspoon garlic salt

Mix the cereals, pretzels and nuts together. Melt the butter and add the seasonings. Pour over the cereal mixture. Bake in a large deep tray. (I borrow one of my husband's porcelain photographic trays. It is 12 x 15 x 2½ inches.)

One half of the above ingredients may be made on a large cookie sheet. Bake in a 250°F. oven for about 2 hours, stirring occasionally. Store in tins and serve as an appetizer or with sour cream dip as an hors d'oeuvre. These may be stored for several weeks.

Artichokes

Select two fresh artichokes at your produce market. Trim the leaves and tie the tops with string. Cook until just tender in a pressure cooker (3 minutes at 15 pounds pressure). Chill thoroughly. Place on a pretty tray with a dish of **Homemade mayonnaise** between them. Dash tarragon on the mayonnaise. In summer serve with cold herb tea.

Cheese Roll

2 8-ounce packages cream cheese
1 small jar soft cheddar cheese (sharp)
1 small jar roka cheese
½ cup chopped pecans
½ teaspoon garlic salt

Blend all the cheeses until very smooth. Shape in balls, rolls, rectangles or squares as desired (one-fourth of mixture for each). Spread the chopped pecans and garlic salt on a sheet of waxed paper. Roll the cheese in the pecans, coating well. Serve with hardtack, wheat crackers or thinly-sliced black rye bread and individual wooden spreaders.

Don't pass judgment on this until you've tried it. It is delicious!

Man-pleasing Dip
1 CUP

½ cup peanut butter (creamy or crunchy)
½ cup chili sauce
4 strips very crisp bacon

Blend the peanut butter and chili sauce until very smooth. Crumble the bacon into the mixture and blend slightly. Serve with a variety of thin crackers.

These are delicious and can be made ahead and frozen. Shape and put into two plastic freezer bags, one inside the other.

Crisp Cheese Balls
ABOUT 2 DOZEN

6 ounces sharp Wisconsin cheddar cheese, grated
¼ cup butter
½ cup sifted unbleached flour
¼ teaspoon sea salt
¼ teaspoon paprika
1 cup cornflakes

Blend the cheese and butter. Add the flour and seasonings, then the cornflakes. Mix well with your hands until the mixture will hold together. Pinch off small bits and roll into bite-sized balls. Bake on an ungreased cookie sheet at 375°F. for 10 or 12 minutes.

Chicken Wing Appetizers
SERVES 4

20 chicken wings (about 3 or 4 pounds)
½ cup soy sauce
¼ cup butter
¼ cup catsup
2 tablespoons wild honey

Chicken wings have 2 joints (3 meaty sections). The tips are not to be used for this dish, so cut them off and save for chicken stock. Cut the remaining wings at the joint. You now have 40 small, drumstick-like chicken pieces. Wash and pat dry with paper towels. Blend the sauce ingredients and heat. Coat each wing piece with the sauce and place on a lined cookie sheet. Bake in a preheated 350°F. oven for 1 hour. Turn once. When crispy brown, serve with the remaining sauce on the side. Be sure to give everyone a heated damp cloth *(oshibori)* because these are very messy. They are also delicious served cold for a buffet or picnic.

These clams are especially good as appetite tantalizers before a fish entrée. For a main course, just double the recipe.

Baked Stuffed Clams
SERVES 4-6

25 butter clams
1 cup bread crumbs
½ small onion, chopped fine
½ teaspoon sage or poultry seasoning
sea salt and pepper to taste
2 tablespoons melted butter
juice from cooking clams

Steam the clams in enough water to cover until they open; reserve the broth. Clean and save the shells. Grind the clams, using the finest blade of a food grinder. Mix all the ingredients, adding a bit of the clam broth so the mixture will hold together. Rub the clam shells with enough butter to coat them. Heap the clam mixture into the shells. Bake in a preheated 350°F. oven for 30 minutes. Serve with oyster forks.

Grandmother's Cheese Dreams

1 pound cheddar cheese, grated
½ cup cream
1 tablespoon Worcestershire sauce
2 egg whites, well beaten
sea salt and pepper to taste
½ teaspoon Tabasco sauce
¼ teaspoon (or less) garlic salt

Mix all the ingredients together into a paste and refrigerate. Just before serving as an hors d'oeuvre, spread generously between slices of good whole-wheat bread and grill in butter in a skillet or sandwich grill. When well-browned, cut each sandwich twice diagonally, making four. Serve with small glasses of very cold Chablis.

This sensational dip from south of the border may be found in most food markets, but the commercially-made product cannot compare with one made from the following authentic recipe. It is among the most deliciously refreshing dips we have found anywhere.

Guacamole Dip
ABOUT 2 CUPS

2 well ripened avocados
2 tablespoons freshly squeezed lime juice
1 small clove garlic, minced
¼ teaspoon sea salt
½ large red onion, chopped
¼ teaspoon chili powder
1 small-to-medium tomato, cut into eighths

Peel the avocados, remove the pits and mash in a bowl. Add the lime juice (lemon juice may be substituted). Add the garlic, salt, onion, chili powder and tomato. Cover and chill thoroughly. Place one of the avocado pits into the center for decoration (it will also prevent the dip from discoloring). Serve with fresh **Tortilla chips.**

Tortilla Chips

The prepackaged tortilla chips available in food markets are certainly acknowledged to be easier and more convenient in every way, but flavor and assurance of freshness is guaranteed only by preparing in your own kitchen. It is remarkably easy and well worth the effort. Buy prepared corn tortillas and cut the entire dozen of the package at one cutting into 8 equal triangles. Preheat safflower, corn, sesame or soy oil to 375° in a large skillet. Carefully drop in single tortilla sections, cooking about a dozen at a time. When done, drain on absorbent paper towels, lightly salt and serve immediately with a favorite dip.

Cheese Tortillas with Green Chili Salsa Sauce

Grate cheddar or jack cheese and sprinkle generously over tortilla chips spread out evenly on an ungreased cookie sheet. Heat in a hot oven (425°F.) until the cheese is melted. Top with small amounts of salsa sauce.

Salsa Sauce

6 medium tomatoes

1, 2 or 3 green chili peppers (depending on how hot you want the sauce)

¼ cup minced onion

½ teaspoon salt

¼ teaspoon paprika

Peel and finely cut the tomatoes, chili peppers and onion. Add seasonings and store in a jar in the refrigerator.

These little one-bite goodies will cause a certain stir when served as an hors d'oeuvre or color accent to a dinner salad. A few of them, if left over, are very nutritious in the youngster's lunch box.

Stuffed Tomatoes

2 hard-cooked eggs, grated

3 tablespoons Homemade mayonnaise

1 teaspoon mustard

½ teaspoon onion salt

½ teaspoon sea salt

¼ teaspoon paprika

20 small cherry tomatoes

    paprika

    parsley (optional)

    carrot sticks (optional)

    green pepper slices (optional)

Make egg salad by mixing the eggs with the mayonnaise, mustard, onion salt and ¼ teaspoon paprika. With a very sharp knife cut an X on the top of each tomato. Gently open and fill with egg salad until it mounds up. Sprinkle paprika on top and serve on a platter surrounded by parsley, carrot sticks, and green pepper slices.

Raw vegetables not only have all their vitamins and minerals intact, but are really delicious. Colorfully spread on a large platter along with a creamy dip, they present a very interesting introduction to the meal to come.

Vegetable Platter Hors d'Oeuvre

broccoli	scallions
turnips	squash
carrots	green beans
peppers	beets (thinly sliced)
cucumbers	sweet potatoes
celery	radishes
tomato wedges	cauliflower florets

Wash well but do not peel any or all of the vegetables listed above.

Cut into easy-to-handle pieces and arrange with parsley on the platter around a **Creamy dip** or **Gaucamole.**

Creamy Dip
1 CUP

1 cup cottage cheese
1 tablespoon lemon juice
sea salt and pepper
onion salt (optional)
garlic salt (optional)
cream

Put the ingredients into a blender until very smooth and creamy. Add a little cream.

Homemade Peanut Butter

Making your own peanut butter is fun and assures you that it is the freshest available.

Use any amount from 1 to 6 cups of shelled freshly roasted peanuts (cashews are also very good). Put into the blender, adding a small amount of sesame oil as the peanuts blend. Add a touch of salt. Homemade peanut butter will separate in the jar after a while. If it does, just stir it up.

Yummy Rolls
MAKES 12

Spread **Homemade peanut butter** (see above) evenly on 12 slices of thin bacon. Roll up and secure with a toothpick. Brown slowly in a skillet until crisp. Drain and serve warm.

Shrimp Spread
ABOUT 1 CUP

½ cup butter
½ to ¾ cup baby shrimp
¼ teaspoon sea salt

Mix all the ingredients in a blender until smooth. Spread on toast rounds. Accent with a tiny sliver of pimiento or red bell pepper. This is also very good spread on thin-sliced bread as a finger sandwich.

Avoid the nitrate and nitrite versions of the hot dog. Shop at your local health food store for pure all-meat varieties available there.

Hot Dog!

½ cup chili sauce
½ cup grape jelly (preferably from organically-grown grapes
4 frankfurters

Heat the chili sauce and jelly in a pan. Slice the frankfurters into tiny rounds and add to the heated sauce. Keep warm over a warmer and have an ample supply of toothpicks handy.

Ramaki

Wrap chicken livers with thin slices of bacon and bake in a preheated 400°F. oven until the bacon is crisp. Drain. Spear with toothpicks and serve warm.

This is easy for the new bride—and easy on the groom's pocketbook.

Newlywed's Pâté

1 8-ounce package liverwurst
¼ cup sweet butter
1 3-ounce package cream cheese
¼ teaspoon sea salt
⅛ teaspoon white pepper

Blend all the ingredients in the blender until smooth and creamy. Pack into a serving dish and store in the refrigerator for several days. Serve with wheat thins or Scandinavian rye crisp crackers. For canapés, top each with a thin slice of raw mushroom. If the groom takes his lunch to work, start his nutrition off right with a sandwich of this pâté, a variety of fresh vegetable chunks or slices, an orange and a thermos of organic grape juice.

The foregoing hors d'oeuvres and canapés of the New World are but a fraction of those available, but in our opinion are among the easiest and best.

Where would we be without soup?

There is nothing more inviting after a healthy hike in the woods, a skiing expedition, a romp in the snow, a session chopping firewood or any other outdoor activity than a steaming hot savory-good bowl of one's favorite soup. Not only is it warming and tasty, but properly made can be one of the most nutritious pleasures of the day. Soups can

be the start of a meal, the end of a meal, or indeed the meal itself. They can be very simple or very elaborate. In our travels we have enjoyed a great variety of soups and in each instance have sought to record the best. We hope you agree with us on the selection.

Parsley is a universal herb. It can be used to enhance almost any recipe, as a garnish, or as an integral part of the dish itself. This parsley soup recipe takes advantage of its versatility.

Parsley Soup
SERVES 4

2 medium potatoes
¼ cup butter
1 quart chicken stock or broth
1 large bunch fresh parsley
1 large onion, chopped
1 teaspoon sea salt
¼ teaspoon pepper
⅛ teaspoon garlic salt or a bit of crushed clove
¼ cup freshly chopped chives
2 cups milk
    parsley and chopped chives for garnish

Wash, peel and dice the potatoes. Cook in a covered saucepan with the butter and ¼ cup of the chicken stock until tender. Put into a blender to puree. Wash the parsley and remove the thick stems. Add to the potatoes and puree. (Add a bit more chicken stock if necessary.) Add the onion and the seasonings. Puree, adding the remainder of the chicken stock. Put into the top of a double boiler and heat. Gradually stir in the milk. When ready to serve, top with a bit of chopped chives and a hint of parsley.

We first discovered this flavor delight in Mexico, but now enjoy it made in our own kitchen. It is a low-cost dish and because of the variety of ingredients and filling quality, it can serve as an entire meal, accompanied by warmed tortillas spread with sweet butter or **Cheese butter.** *Organic citrus juice or limeade is a delicious complement as the beverage. The meatballs may be varied by substituting pine nut for the rice. Chopped olives or pimientos add additional color and flavor.*

Albóndigas
(Mexican meatball soup)

1 small yellow onion
1 medium carrot
1 medium tomato
1 quart beef stock or consommé
  sea salt and pepper to taste
1 bay leaf
¾ pound lean ground beef
1 tablespoon chopped onion
2 eggs
2 tablespoons uncooked brown rice
¼ teaspoon chili powder
1 tablespoon cilantro* (optional)
  sea salt and pepper

Peel and dice the onion. Scrape the carrot and cut into small pieces. Mash the tomato. Add these to the beef stock along with the seasonings and bay leaf. Cook, covered, until steaming and bubbling.

Mix the remaining ingredients and form into small balls. Carefully drop these into the simmering broth, one at a time. Lower the heat and simmer for about 40 minutes. Remove the bay leaf and serve at once.

An interesting variation is to add a scant ¼ cup of sherry to the soup just before serving.

*The herb cilantro is usually found in Chinese specialty markets, although large supermarkets and health food stores occasionally have it. If you would enjoy growing your own, plant coriander seed, which closely resembles parsley but has a quite different taste. This soup is excellent without cilantro but more authentic when it is included.

Aduki beans can be found in most health food stores. They may be sprouted for use in salads, also.

Aduki Bean Soup

1 cup aduki beans
3 cups water
½ cup chopped scallions
1 teaspoon sea salt

Put the beans and water into a pressure cooker and cook at 10 pounds pressure for 1 hour. Put in the blender and puree. Return to the pot and add the scallions and salt. Simmer for 30 to 40 minutes. Be sure to add the salt last since cooking in the pressure cooker has a tendency to toughen the beans. Serve with warmed black bread and butter.

Scotch Broth

1 pound lamb or beef shank

1 quart water

2 carrots

1 small onion

⅟ cup chopped fresh tomatoes

¼ cup barley

1 teaspoon sea salt

1 tablespoon finely chopped fresh parsley

Put all the ingredients into a large pot and simmer, covered, for 3 hours. Remove the meat, cut into very small pieces, and return to the pot. Reheat about an hour before serving. (If the soup is refrigerated overnight, the fat may be easily removed before reheating.)

This is one of our favorite simmer soups. Simmer for about 8 hours . . . or more. The longer, the better!

Vim and Vigor Remedy Soup

1½ quarts water

1 veal knuckle

1 beef knuckle

1 pound neck bones or lean beef

2 beets with tops

2 carrots with tops

¼ pound spinach

¼ pound okra

¼ pound green beans

½ pound zucchini

½ cup fresh parsley

¼ cup green peas

¼ cup Chinese peas

¼ cup barley

1 teaspoon sea salt

¼ cup white vinegar

Put all the ingredients into a large pot and simmer . . . simmer . . . simmer. This is an extremely well-balanced variety of nature's finest vitamins and minerals in liquified form. The softened vegetables are not difficult to digest or severe in any way to a convalescent. Always add a bit more water each time it is reheated. This legendary remedy soup has been long known as the way to "put a man back on the plow in a jiffy."

The early memory of the fragrance of this delicious chicken soup drifting up the stairs to the child lying in bed with a sniffle, lasts for life. Maybe it is the loving attention that accompanies the soup, as well as the taste. In any case, it's hard to beat.

Chicken Soup

1 stewing chicken, 4 to 5 pounds
3 quarts water
1 teaspoon sea salt
 juice of ½ lemon
2 cloves
2 small onions
1 small carrot
2 stalks celery
3 sprigs parsley

Simmer the chicken in the water with the salt and lemon juice until the chicken is very tender, about 1½ or 2 hours. Remove the chicken, take the meat from the bones, and cut into bite-sized pieces. Strain the broth and return the meat to it. Stick a clove into each onion and add to the broth (this makes the cloves easy to find and remove later). Dice the carrot, celery and parsley. Simmer for at least 2 hours. Strain and serve the broth.

This recipe was given to us by the curator of the museum at Sheldon Jackson College, Sitka, Alaska. While there, we asked a native which were the best Alaskan clams. "Why, the ones you've just gathered," was the answer. There are more than two hundred varieties to be found in Alaskan waters. Since we don't have the chance to gather our own, we just ask our fish market for "Alaskan clams, please."

Alaskan Clam Chowder

2 cups clams
1-inch cube salt pork, diced
1 small onion, chopped fine
½ cup unbleached flour
   sea salt and pepper to taste
1 large potato, cut into small cubes
2 cups water
2 cups milk
¼ cup butter

Steam the clams in enough water to cover until they open, then clean. Strain off the liquid and save ½ cup. Dice the clams, perhaps leaving one or two whole for a garnish. In a large skillet brown the bits of salt pork until crisp. Drain and set aside. Brown the onions in the same pan. Put the flour, salt and pepper into a small brown paper bag, then put in the potatoes and clams. Shake well to coat thoroughly. Add to the pot. Have 2 cups of water boiling and pour over the ingredients in the pot. Simmer stirring until the potatoes are tender, about 30 minutes. Heat the milk with the butter and add while stirring. Mix about 1 tablespoon of the butter and flour with the clam broth and blend. Add last to thicken the soup before serving.

Put a few crisp pork bits into the bottom of each bowl at serving time. (Bacon, well-crisped, may be substituted with good results.)

Alaskan Pink Cream
(Salmon Cream Soup)
SERVES 4 AS THE MAIN
DISH, 8 AS A
SOUP COURSE

1 to 1½ pounds fresh salmon
2 cups hot water
1 quart milk
2 tablespoons finely chopped onion
1 stalk celery, diced
1 sprig parsley, chopped fine
⅓ cup butter
⅓ cup unbleached flour
   sea salt and pepper to taste
½ teaspoon paprika
   parsley or paprika for garnish

Remove the skin and bones from the salmon and grind twice using the finest blade of a good grinder. Stir the salmon into the hot water and gently simmer for about 5 minutes, stirring constantly. Mix 1 cup of the milk with the onion, celery and parsley. Puree in the blender. Add the remaining milk and bring to a boil. Skim off the froth and discard. Blend the butter, flour and seasonings together and slowly stir into the hot milk mixture. When somewhat thickened, add the salmon, heat a bit and serve, sprinkled with parsley bits or paprika. For a more elegant presentation, whip 1 cup of heavy cream, blend lightly with ½ teaspoon paprika, and put a pale-pink dollop of the fluffy cream in the center of each bowl of soup. Serve with warmed brown bread and whipped sweet butter.

Soups are so popular around our house that we keep a supply on hand at all times in the refrigerator or the freezer. Stocks will keep very well for several weeks when refrigerated and indefinitely in the freezer. We usually freeze in three different container sizes: quarts for soups, pints for smaller soup recipes and sauces, one cup for smaller sauce recipes or one serving soups. This system is convenient and thrifty. If you have a large enough pot, this recipe may be doubled.

Kettle of Stock

2 pounds beef marrow bones

2 pounds veal bones (or steak bones)

2 whole cloves

10 whole black peppercorns

1 bay leaf

1 sprig lemon thyme

4 quarts water

2 carrots, diced

1 large onion, sliced

1 stalk celery, diced

parsley

½ small white turnip

1 pound lean ground beef

Brown the bones in a pan in the oven at 375°F. for about 1½ hours. Put the cloves, peppercorns, bay leaf and thyme in a small cloth bag. Cook all the vegetables in the water along with the ground meat and spice bag. As soon as the bones in the oven are well browned, add them to the simmering pot. After 8 hours of simmering, strain through a cloth and cool. This stock will add a delightful flavor to any recipe calling for broth.

We are conservative and can't stand the thought of discarding the remnants of this broth stock. We discard the bones, bay leaf and spice bag. Everything else finds its way into various other dishes such as casseroles.

Stock
Casserole

Cook enough spinach noodles or whole-wheat noodles for four in 2 quarts of salted water. Layer in a buttered casserole dish with the leftovers from the stock just made (see above). Add 2 cups of the liquid stock that has been mixed with 2 tablespoons each flour and butter. Pour over the noodle mixture and top with a good natural cheese. Bake for 1 hour in a preheated 300°F. oven.

Cheese
Soup

2 tablespoons chopped onion

1 tablespoon chopped green pepper

2 tablespoons chopped carrot

4 tablespoons butter

3 tablespoons unbleached flour

1 quart chicken broth or stock

2 cups grated Cheddar cheese (or your favorite sharp variety)

1 cup milk

sea salt and pepper to taste

In a large pot brown the vegetables in butter until tender (about 10 minutes), stirring constantly. Mix the flour with a little of the chicken broth, then blend in with the rest of the broth. Pour over the vegetables. Mix the grated cheese with the milk and seasonings and add, stirring, until the cheese is melted and piping hot. Serve with additional grated cheese on top.

This soup is very rich and flavorful, so you will probably want to serve only a small bowl to begin a meal. As a main course serve with a small leafy salad, warm bread and butter.

Almond Soup

1 heaping tablespoon butter
1 heaping tablespoon flour
3 cups chicken broth or stock
¼ cup ground almonds
   sea salt and white pepper to taste
½ cup heavy cream
1 tablespoon finely chopped celery leaves

Blend the butter and flour in a saucepan until smooth. Add the chicken broth and stir over a low heat until blended and thickened. Add the almonds to the hot mixture. Season with salt and white pepper. Remove from the fire and add the cream. Cover and let stand for 30 minutes. This steeps out the almond flavor. Reheat to serve, topped with the celery leaves.

In the downtown area of Nashville, Tennessee, there was at one time a very fine restaurant which featured an outstanding and unique bill-of-fare. A childhood favorite was this **Cracker ball soup.**

Cracker Ball Soup

1 quart chicken stock
½ teaspoon marjoram
   handful of green onion tops
3 tops of celery, carrots
4 eggs slightly beaten
5 tablespoons water
   (4½ eggshells full)
3 tablespoons chicken fat (skimmed off top of chicken broth)
1 teaspoon minced parsley
   salt and pepper to taste
   cracker crumbs to make a thick paste
   dash of nutmeg

Put the chicken stock and marjoram in a pot to begin heating. Tie the onion, celery and carrot tops together with string and put in the pot. Simmer very slowly over a low heat. Blend the eggs, water, chicken fat, parsley, salt, pepper and nutmeg. Add enough cracker crumbs to this mixture to make a thick paste. Form into balls about 2 inches in diameter. Put these into the soup and simmer for about 30 minutes. Use a slotted spoon to ease the balls into the soup so they will keep their shape. Remove the bundle of tops and put 1 or 2 cracker balls into each soup bowl and ladle the soup in over them.

This delightful Italian treat developed out of the practice of keeping a large steaming pot on the piers of Italian fishing villages. Returning fishermen might toss several items of their catch and later join into a communal supper, with large bowls passed around to everyone.

It is a marvelous dinner for a large group, although somewhat messy since it is literally eaten with the hands along with thick slices of fresh-baked bread. Be sure to supply everyone with a protective bib. Double or triple this recipe for a large gathering.

Cioppino

1 large crab, cleaned, cracked and disjointed

½ pound medium shrimp in the shell

6 clams in the shell (refuse to buy an "open" clam!)

6 oysters in the shell

½ pound scallops

½ pound halibut or cod

⅓ cup chopped onion

⅓ cup chopped green pepper

2 tablespoons olive oil (safflower, sesame or corn oil may be substituted)

1 clove garlic, crushed

1 quart tomato juice

1 cup dry white wine

1 fresh peeled tomato

¼ teaspoon oregano

¼ teaspoon basil

¼ teaspoon paprika

¼ teaspoon raw sugar

½ teaspoon thyme

1 bay leaf

pinch of saffron

Clean and prepare all seafood. Set aside and prepare the sauce. In a large kettle (at least 4-quart) saute the onion, green pepper and garlic in the olive oil. When they are limp add tomato juice and wine. Simmer 5 minutes. Add tomato cut into small pieces, then all spices. Cover and simmer 15 minutes. Drop all seafood into the boiling liquid. Simmer another 15 minutes until all is tender. Pour into a large soup tureen and serve at the table. Provide everyone with a large bowl, bib, bread and butter. If you did not recover the bay leaf during serving remind everyone to look out for it. Cioppino is one of the finest ethnic legacies from the Old World, now a comfortable part of New World nutrition.

This cold soup originated in Spain where it was thought of as a peasant soup. It is often served in Mexico as a part of its Spanish heritage. The main difference in recipes between the two countries is the addition of lime juice in Mexico.

Gazpacho

2 tablespoons olive oil

2 tablespoons lemon juice

3 cups tomato juice

1 cup chicken broth or stock

2 tomatoes, peeled and cubed

¼ cup finely chopped onion

¼ cup finely chopped celery

¼ teaspoon Tabasco sauce

1 teaspoon salt

¼ teaspoon ground pepper

2 tablespoons bread crumbs

1 green pepper, chopped fine, chilled

1 red onion, chopped fine, chilled

1 cucumber, chopped fine, chilled

croutons

Beat the oil and lemon juice together. Stir in the remaining ingredients except green peppers, red onion, cucumber and croutons. If you use the blender, the soup will have a smoother texture. Chill for at least 3 hours before serving. Combine with the remainder of the ingredients at serving time and let everyone help themselves from a large tureen, topping with crunchy croutons. This delightful Spanish soup is particularly good on a warm day, but we enjoy it equally in the dead of winter before an open fire.

A full serving contains only about 60 calories.

Fresh Mushroom Low-calorie Soup

2 tablespoons finely minced onion

1 tablespoon sweet butter

2 cups chicken broth or stock

2 cups skim milk

   sea salt and pepper to taste

1 pound large fresh mushrooms, thinly sliced

1 tablespoon sherry (optional)

Cook the onions in the butter until limp but not browned. Add all the other ingredients except the mushrooms and sherry and simmer for ½ hour or more. About 10 minutes before serving, add the mushrooms and cook until just tender. A tablespoon of sherry may be added just before serving.

Salads

Inasmuch as salads are a favored fare at our house, we have many varieties that are exciting, inventive, delicious and above all, nutritious.

An elaborate salad with a variety of lettuce, raw vegetables and tempting meats teamed with a good dressing can be an entire meal.

Small salads, simple in their texture and flavor, provide a perfect liaison between the appetizers and the main course. In any case salads are an excellent source of many vitamins, minerals and roughage.

*Four-
bean
Salad*

1 small red onion
½ cup celery
1 small green pepper
1 cup cooked green beans
1 cup cooked yellow waxed beans
1 cup cooked kidney beans
1 cup cooked garbanzo beans
⅓ cup raw sugar
1 teaspoon sea salt
1 teaspoon pepper
½ cup wine vinegar or cider vinegar
½ cup polyunsaturated oil

Chop the onion, celery, and green pepper finely. Mix with the beans, seasonings and oil. Cover and refrigerate overnight. Serve in individual bowls or on a large lettuce leaf. Great for picnics and school lunches.

There aren't too many lettuce salads that may be prepared ahead of time with any degree of success, but here is one that will stand up to the test. This is easy and delicious.

*Layer
Lettuce
Salad*

1 quart volume of lettuce (your choice)
1 small red onion, thinly sliced
1 cup natural Swiss cheese, cut into tiny strips
1 cup cooked tiny green peas
⅔ cup Homemade mayonnaise
2 tablespoons raw sugar
sea salt and pepper to taste

Layer the lettuce, onion, Swiss cheese, green peas and mayonnaise, sprinkling a bit of sugar as you go. Cover and chill for 3 hours, or longer. At serving time toss at the table and season to taste.

Festive Holiday Salad
SERVES 4

4 red apples
1 teaspoon cinnamon
1 cup walnut halves or pieces
1 cup heavy cream
2 tablespoons raw sugar
½ teaspoon vanilla

Peel the apples but leave several strips of red peeling for decoration. Cut into bite-sized pieces. Mix apple pieces with cinnamon and nuts. Whip the cream and add sugar and vanilla. Fold all together gently. Serve in a bright red bowl for a holiday flair. A small pine cone or sprig of fir sets this off attractively.

Sprout Salad
SERVES 4

2 cups bean sprouts
½ cup sliced fresh mushrooms
¼ cup diced red and green peppers
¼ cup diced celery
¼ cup diced onion
½ cup slivered meat or fish

Toss all the ingredients together and serve with the following **Oil and lemon dressing.**

Oil and Lemon Dressing

2 tablespoons lemon juice
3 tablespoons polyunsaturated oil
herb seasoning
sea salt and pepper

Beat lemon juice and oil together and season to taste with herb seasoning and a dash of salt and pepper. Toss dressing into the salad and chill thoroughly before serving.

Homemade Bean Sprouts

Homemade bean sprouts are even more delicious with this salad and obviously fresher. If you don't have time for the 4 or 5-day growing period, they may be bought in most markets. Don't use the canned variety, they don't taste nearly the same.

There are many good seeds and beans suitable for producing homemade bean sprouts. Your own tastes will be satisfied only after trying several types. First try mung beans or fenugreek seeds.

Place 1 tablespoon of fenugreek seeds or 2 tablespoons mung beans in a quart jar. Fill to the halfway point with water. Soak overnight. The following morning drain off the water and cover the mouth of the jar with cheesecloth or nylon netting held tightly over the opening with a rubber band. Lay the jar on its side in a dark kitchen cabinet. The following morning irrigate the seeds or beans with water (fill and pour out of the jar). Return to the cabinet. Repeat this process each morning. On the fifth day the sprouts should be fully matured. Rinse and pinch off the seed or bean hulls and rinse, then store in the refrigerator for 3 to 5 days, or use immediately. The seed hulls may be left on for added flavor. These are not only very nutritious but also fun for the children or grandchildren who participate in the project. It is a great way to put across the idea of how living plants grow and foods develop.

Apricot Nectar Salad

1 cup fresh peach slices
1 tablespoon lemon juice
1 cup cantaloupe balls (or bite-sized pieces)
1 12-ounce bottle organic apricot nectar
1 package lemon gelatin

Dip the peach slices into the lemon juice to prevent turning brown. Mix with the cantaloupe and put into a dish or mold. Heat the nectar and stir in the gelatin until dissolved. Pour this over the fruit in the mold. Chill until firm. Serve with the following **Fresh Dressing.**

This is very good on any gelatin or fruit salad.

Fresh Dressing
SERVES 4

½ cup raw sugar
2 tablespoons unbleached flour
1 egg, slightly beaten
  juice of ½ lemon
⅓ cup pineapple juice
2 tablespoons melted butter
¼ teaspoon sea salt
½ cup heavy cream

Combine the sugar and flour and add to the egg. Mix the lemon and pineapple juices, butter and salt. Cook in the top of a double boiler over medium heat until thick. Cool. Whip the cream and gently fold in.

This recipe may be doubled or quadrupled.

Cole Slaw with Honey-cream Dressing

1 medium head cabbage
1 cup sour cream
2 tablespoons honey
1 teaspoon vinegar
½ teaspoon sea salt
1 teaspoon celery salt
⅛ teaspoon freshly ground pepper

Shred the cabbage. Store in the refrigerator while making the dressing. Mix all the other ingredients together in a bowl. Blend thoroughly with a wire whisk and pour over the cabbage. Toss and serve immediately.

Wilted Spinach Salad

1 pound fresh spinach
1 hard-cooked egg, grated
¼ cup chopped green onions or Bermuda onion
¼ teaspoon dry mustard
¼ teaspoon paprika
¼ teaspoon sea salt
¼ teaspoon raw sugar
4 slices bacon

Wash the spinach and drain on absorbent towels (a little salt in the water will help loosen any clinging dirt). Mix the spinach with the grated egg and onion. Add the seasonings and toss. Fry the bacon until crisp and drain. Save the drippings. Break the bacon into bits over the spinach. Add 2 tablespoons of the bacon drippings to ½ cup prepared Italian salad dressing and ⅛ cup water. Heat to high boil and pour over the spinach mixture. Toss and serve immediately.

Avocado and Shrimp Salad
SERVES 4

2 ripe avocados
1 cup small cooked shrimp
½ cup chopped celery
1 teaspoon lemon juice
½ cup Homemade yogurt

Peel and cut avocados in half. Remove pit. Mix the shrimp and celery with the lemon juice. Fold in the yogurt and mound in equal portions on the avocado halves.

Fruit Hawaiian

1 cup mandarin orange slices
1 cup fresh pineapple chunks (or canned)
1 cup seedless grapes
1 cup strawberries
¼ cup grated coconut
1 pint sour cream
1 cup sliced bananas
1 tablespoon lemon juice

Mix all the fruit except the bananas with sour cream and chill overnight, or at least 12 hours. Just before serving add the bananas and lemon juice.

Tomato-Cheese Mold

1 tablespoon unflavored gelatin
½ cup cold water
1 11-ounce can cream of tomato soup, undiluted
1 3-ounce package cream cheese
½ cup Homemade mayonnaise
½ teaspoon sea salt
1 tablespoon lemon juice
1 tablespoon grated onion
½ cup chopped celery

Soak the gelatin in water for 10 minutes. Heat soup and stir into softened gelatin. Beat the cream cheese with the mayonnaise until well blended. Slowly add the soup mixture. Add the remaining ingredients and blend thoroughly. Pour into a ring mold that has been lightly brushed with cooking oil and rinsed in cold water. Chill until firm. Unmold and serve on a bed of lettuce leaves with bits of fresh parsley for accent.

Yogurt is a thick, semisolid dairy food with good food value and taste. It is low in fat and high in protein. Since the yogurt is a fermented culture of bacteria, once you have made it you may continue to culture new batches as needed. Always save 2 tablespoons to use as a starter for a fresh batch. Yogurt is not only very inexpensive but also easy to make as well.

Homemade Yogurt

1 quart skim milk (I prefer certified raw, but commercial is acceptable)

2 tablespoons plain yogurt from your market

Heat the milk in a saucepan until it begins to bubble. Remove from the fire and let stand until it is at room temperature. Stir in the 2 table-spoons yogurt and mix well with a wire whisk. Pour this into a large Pyrex bowl and put in the oven. The oven temperature should not be more than 150°F. Leave for 8 hours. Store in the refrigerator and use as yogurt, plain or with desserts and salads. This retains its flavor and nutritional value for a week.

This is quickest and easiest made in the blender.

Homemade Mayonnaise
1¼ CUPS

1 whole egg

1 egg yolk

2 tablespoons tarragon or cider vinegar

¼ teaspoon dry mustard

½ teaspoon sea salt

1 cup polyunsaturated vegetable oil

Put all ingredients except the oil into the blender. Mix well. Remove the small top of the blender and very slowly pour in the oil. After the last of the oil has been added the mayonnaise should be quite thick. Refrigerate and enjoy on anything where mayonnaise is used.

Honey Dressing
FOR FRUIT

⅔ cup raw sugar

1 teaspoon dry mustard

1 teaspoon paprika

¼ teaspoon celery salt

1 teaspoon celery seed

½ cup honey

5 tablespoons cider vinegar

1 tablespoon lemon juice

1 teaspoon grated onion

1 cup salad oil

Mix the dry ingredients. Add the remaining ingredients with the exception of the oil. Pour in the oil slowly, beating constantly. Refrigerate.

This can be great fun for a simple lunch of fruit pieces served in individual bowls. Place a chilled bowl of this dressing within reach for dipping the fruit, and you have a fruit fondue.

Refrigerator French Dressing
ABOUT 2 PINTS

1 medium onion, grated

1 clove garlic, chopped fine

1½ cups salad oil

1 tablespoon prepared mustard

1 tablespoon steak sauce

1 tablespoon horseradish

2 tablespoons capers, mashed

1 teaspoon paprika

1 teaspoon sea salt

1 teaspoon pepper

⅓ cup cider vinegar

1 11-ounce can cream of tomato soup

Mix all the ingredients together and beat with a rotary egg beater until smooth. It will be rich, creamy and have a slight gloss.

Roquefort cheese is considerably stronger in taste and more expensive to buy than blue cheese. Either is delicious for salads so it is really a matter of choice.

Roquefort or Blue-cheese Dressing

1 cup fresh buttermilk

3 tablespoons lemon juice

2 cups Homemade mayonnaise

½ pound Roquefort or blue cheese, crumbled into pieces

1 clove garlic, put through a press

1 tablespoon finely chopped parsley

½ teaspoon sea salt

¼ teaspoon coarsely ground pepper

1 teaspoon Worcestershire sauce

Chill the buttermilk and add lemon juice. Beat with a wire whisk until thick in texture. Add all other ingredients and blend well. Store, covered, in the refrigerator for weeks. Ladle generous amounts of the dressing over orange and grapefruit sections with avocado slices on a bed of lettuce. Serve with rye grain crackers.

Thousand-Island Dressing

Combine 1¼ cups of **Homemade mayonnaise** with ¼ cup chili sauce.

Tomato and Sprout Salad
SERVES 4

2 medium tomatoes, sliced thin

4 tablespoons cottage cheese

1 cup alfalfa sprouts (make your own if you have the time)

1 tablespoon chopped parsley

1 teaspoon freshly chopped sweet basil

½ small carrot, grated

¾ cup tuna or cooked chicken or cooked fish

sesame seeds for garnish

Layer this salad on lettuce. Accent with sesame seeds.

Chicken Salad

¼ cup crisply-fried chicken skin

½ small head lettuce

½ cup brown rice, cooked and chilled

1 tablespoon freshly chopped parsley

2 tablespoons chopped green onions

½ teaspoon sea salt

¼ cup Homemade mayonnaise

¼ cup chopped toasted almonds

Remove the skin from a chicken. Cut the skin into ½-inch wide pieces. Fry quickly until crispy and drain.

Shred the lettuce and toss with all the other ingredients. The chicken skin should be tossed in just at serving time. This crispy hint of chicken adds a subtle flavor.

Twenty-four-hour Green-bean Salad

3 cups whole green beans (the smaller, the better)
1 red onion, thinly sliced
⅓ cup raw sugar
1 cup cider vinegar
3 tablespoons sesame oil
4 tablespoons Refrigerator French dressing

Cook beans and set aside, reserving ⅓ cup of the liquid. Layer the beans and onion slices in a deep casserole dish. Bring all the other ingredients (including the reserved bean liquid) to a boil and pour over the beans. Let stand at room temperature for 1 hour and then refrigerate for 24 hours. Serve cold.

Stuffed Cucumber Salad

4 small cucumbers
½ cup cooked green peas
4 tablespoons Homemade mayonnaise
1 tablespoon chopped parsley
½ teaspoon chopped tarragon
paprika for garnish

Peel the cucumbers. Cut in half lengthwise and hollow out the center. (Save for blender soups.) Mix the other ingredients and fill the hollows of the cucumbers. A dash of paprika is colorful. Chill thoroughly before serving.

From out of the past

The early explorers, trappers and settlers of the New World left us an interesting food heritage. Without refrigeration or preservation methods and limited by the necessity to travel light, these hardy souls developed a variety of simple foods that were nevertheless nutritious. One classic example is beef jerky, a carefully dried and skillfully preserved meat for the trail. Drying removed the water, thus much of the weight. Notwithstanding the fact that the jerky was stringy, tough and dry, it was very filling and quite good.

While camping on a fast-moving stream in the central interior of British Columbia, Canada, we met a grizzled old prospector. We were panning for gold in the black sands of the stream when we heard a booming voice from the brush behind us, "You'll never get any gold that way!" He approached us and reached for the shiny new gold pan in my hands. "You've got to burn 'em," he stated matter-of-factly.

After brief introductions he explained that the gold pans had a residue of oils left in the metal from manufacturing. He showed us how to "burn" the pans in an open fire. He demonstrated how the fine gold of the sand could be seen against the blackened pan and explained that the oil kept the gold from clinging to the metal.

We had dinner around a roaring campfire as he regaled us with tall tales from the Caribou gold rush. The subject of beef jerky came up and he proudly gave us his recipe. We think it's very good, and nutritious too.

Beef Jerky

10 pounds flank steak

2 quarts water

2 cups salt

2 tablespoons pepper

1 cup cider vinegar

½ cup Worcestershire, soy sauce or steak sauce

Cut the meat across the grain into thin diagonal strips ¼ to ½ inch thick and 1 inch wide (cutting with the grain will produce a chewier jerky). Place the pieces of meat in a large kettle. Pour the water over the meat and add the salt, pepper and vinegar. Slowly bring to a boil. Boil for 1 minute and drain. Lay out the strips on paper towels, cover with more paper towels, and roll with a rolling pin to squeeze out as much water as possible (this will also flatten the meat strips). Put the meat in a warm oven (150°F.) across the oven racks, leaving the door ajar several inches. After 2 hours turn off the heat, open the door fully, and allow to cool. With a pastry brush thoroughly coat the strips with the Worcestershire, soy or steak sauce. Store in tightly-closed jars.

Jerky Stew

8 to 10 strips of jerky

8 small potatoes

4 small white onions

4 small turnips

several carrots

1 cup dark cherries (optional)

Cut up all vegetables into a pot containing a quart of water, slightly salted and add the jerky. Simmer over an open campfire for 2 or 3 hours (or even all day). Add a cup of dark cherries (fresh or canned) an hour before serving for a true pioneer version. Serve with crusty bread and butter.

Recipes with gumbo in the title all stem from the same deep-South heritage, from the bayou country of Louisiana to the Atlantic shores of the Carolinas. Since our family link to the past begins in the South, everyone of the clan has his or her own gumbo specialty. Here is ours.

Creole Gumbo

1 tablespoon butter
1 tablespoon oil
1 clove garlic
1 medium onion, chopped
1 small green pepper, chopped
1 stalk celery, chopped
½ cup diced smoked ham
2 tomatoes, chopped
1 8-ounce can tomato sauce
1 bay leaf
¼ teaspoon paprika
¼ teaspoon basil
¼ teaspoon thyme
   sea salt and pepper to taste
½ cup diced cooked chicken
½ cup raw shrimp, shelled and deveined
½ cup cooked or uncooked lobster
½ cup crab meat
½ cup sliced raw mushrooms

Melt the butter and combine with the oil in a large pot. Press the garlic into this and brown along with the onions, green pepper, celery and ham. Add the tomatoes and tomato sauce, then the seasonings. Simmer for about 30 minutes. Add about 1 cup of water to prevent sticking (but not enough to make the mixture watery). Add the chicken, fish and mushrooms. Simmer until tender (about 15 minutes), adding more water if necessary. At serving time spoon this over cooked brown or wild rice.

Chicken Burgers
SERVES 4

1 chicken (1½ pounds)

1 egg, beaten

1 stalk celery, chopped fine

1 green onion, chopped fine

1 teaspoon Worcestershire sauce

¼ teaspoon freshly ground pepper

½ teaspoon herb seasoning or sea salt

2 tablespoons butter

1 tablespoon chopped parsley

2 tablespoons sour cream

Have the butcher debone the chicken. Grind the meat, using the finest knife of a food grinder. Add the egg along with the celery, onion, and seasonings. Mix well. Shape into patties and sauté in butter for about 10 minutes on each side. Add the parsley to the butter in the pan and stir in the sour cream. Spoon this sauce over the patties.

With inflation a constant problem, this flavor delight wins for economy and goodness.

Unusual Beef Patties
SERVES 4

1 pound ground beef

2 cups uncooked oatmeal

2 tablespoons wheat germ

1 teaspoon sea salt

½ cup milk

1 tablespoon butter

1 tablespoon Worcestershire sauce

1 tablespoon vinegar

1 tablespoon raw sugar

½ cup tomato catsup

¼ cup water

2 medium onions, chopped fine

Mix the meat, oatmeal, wheat germ, salt and milk together. Let stand for 5 minutes. Shape the patties and brown on both sides in butter. Place the patties in a baking dish. Mix all the other ingredients together and pour over the patties. Bake in a preheated 325°F. oven for about 40 minutes. Serve these on slightly toasted honey buns, which may be found in most health food stores or on **Cracked wheat honey buns.** Serve a spoonful of the sauce on each patty.

We encountered this recipe while visiting southern Utah, in the rugged country of the north rim of the Grand Canyon.

Indian Squash or Baked Pumpkin

1 medium pumpkin

½ cup butter

    sea salt and pepper to taste

1 cup corn, cut from the cob

1 cup green beans, cut into 1-inch pieces

1 green pepper, chopped

1 pound lean ground beef

1 yellow onion, chopped

1 cup cooked chicken, cut into small pieces

1 fresh peach

1 apple

½ cup sunflower seeds

¼ teaspoon nutmeg

¼ cup raisins (optional)

Cut the top from the pumpkin as though making a jack-o'-lantern. Scoop out the seeds and stringy membrane. (Save the seeds for roasting). Spread the inside of the pumpkin with butter, salt, and pepper. Set on a cookie sheet, without the top. Bake for about 25 minutes in a preheated 325°F. oven. Check often to see if liquid has built up in the bottom of the pumpkin. If so, remove with a kitchen bulb baster. While the pumpkin is roasting, bake all the other ingredients in a pan for the same amount of time. Remove all liquid in the pumpkin and fill with the vegetable mixture. Put the top on the pumpkin and return to the 325°F. oven for 30 minutes to 1 hour. It is done when the pumpkin is soft and easily pierced with the tines of a fork. Scoop out parts of the pumpkin with each serving.

When we were first married, we lived for a time at Robert's family farm in the central South. The landscape is a gently rolling combination of open fields, cool meadows and dense woods. There were plentiful supplies of various wild game. Quail was a favorite for the table during the hunting season. Lest you pale at the thought of shooting these creatures, consider the fact that they cause damage to certain seed crops of the farming operation.

Roasted Game Birds
SERVES 4

½ cup unbleached flour
sea salt and pepper
2 game birds per person
2 tablespoons butter
4 small onions
4 small tart apples
½ cup apple juice
½ cup water

Put the flour, salt and pepper into a brown paper bag. Put the cleaned birds in and shake to cover with the flour mixture. Melt the butter in a large cast-iron skillet and brown the birds evenly on all sides. Peel and cut the onions and apples into halves. Place the onions and apples with the birds together in the skillet and add the apple juice and water. Bake, covered, in a preheated 275°F. oven until tender, about 1½ hours. Serve with wild or brown rice with apple jelly on the side.

Rock Cornish game hens, while a very fine substitute for the quail, just don't have quite the same unique, delicious flavor.

New England Rarebit
SERVES 4

3 tablespoons butter
3 tablespoons unbleached flour
2 cups milk
1 bouillon cube, crumbled
½ teaspoon sea salt
¼ teaspoon paprika
2 cups grated Cheddar cheese
2 tablespoons cooking sherry
4 English muffins, toasted
12 slices crisply cooked bacon or Canadian bacon

Blend the butter and flour together in a pan over low heat. Add the milk and stir until smooth. Add the seasonings and cheese. When the cheese is melted and the rarebit smooth, add the sherry and serve over English muffins. Top with strips of crisp bacon. (If you want to be terribly English about it, use ale instead of sherry.)

Of the many wonderful family recipes passed down from generation to generation, we truly believe this to be one of the best. Sharing this with you gives us great pleasure.

The aroma of this barbecue sauce is enough to lure perfect strangers in off the street. It takes hours for the full flavor to develop and soak in.

Grandmother's Barbecued Leg of Lamb

5 to 7 pound leg of lamb
sesame oil
sea salt and pepper
unbleached flour

SAUCE
juice of 2 lemons
½ cup vinegar
2 cups water
1 heaping teaspoon mustard
2 tablespoons Worcestershire sauce
1 tablespoon steak sauce
1 medium onion, finely chopped
1 tablespoon brown sugar
1 teaspoon salt
¼ teaspoon pepper

Trim the fat and gristle from the meat. Rub well with oil, then salt and pepper. Dust generously with flour. Sear under the broiler on both sides, finishing with the meaty side up. (If your broiler isn't deep enough to accommodate the lamb, use a large cast-iron skillet.) Mix the sauce ingredients together in a saucepan and bring to a boil, then simmer for 5 minutes.

Cook the lamb in a preheated 250°F. oven for about 4 hours. Baste with the sauce every 15 minutes for the first hour, using all the sauce in four stages. Then baste every ½ hour until done. Remove from the oven. Take a knife and loosen the bone by running the knife edge around it. Take hold of the end and give it a twist. It should slide right out, leaving only the meat. It may be carved at the table as is or cut into small pieces, returned to the sauce and reheated.

For special occasions or for just anytime, remember this: You can prepare this recipe better than 90 percent of the world's best restaurants, and for about one-sixth the cost.

Gayle's Tournedos of Beef
SERVES 4

WINE SAUCE
2 tablespoons finely chopped shallots

2 tablespoons sweet butter

¾ cup rich beef broth

⅓ cup Burgundy wine

1 tablespoon unbleached flour

TOPPING
8 very large fresh mushrooms

1 tablespoon sweet butter

2 tablespoons dry white wine

2 to 3 drops lemon juice

MEAT
1½ pounds filet mignon

¼ cup unbleached flour

sea salt and pepper

Make the wine sauce first. Lightly saute the shallots in the butter. Stir in the broth. Mix the wine and flour together and add, stirring constantly. When the sauce begins to thicken, turn the heat very low.

Now the topping. Clean the mushrooms, cutting off stems. Brown the whole mushrooms in the butter. Add the wine and lemon juice. Cook for 1 minute.

Now the meat. Sprinkle 1 teaspoon salt into a large cast-iron skillet. Slice the filet mignon into 16 equal thin slices. Dust each with flour, salt and pepper. Have the skillet quite hot and sear the filets quickly on both sides. Arrange the slices on a platter. Pour over the hot wine sauce and top with the mushrooms. Serve with wild or brown rice, a simple salad, and red wine. Always have the serving plates well-warmed or use heated steak platters. If this is an intimate dinner for two, cut the proportions in half.

Shallots of your own

Sometimes shallots are difficult to find in the market. To prevent disappointment, buy some when available and split in half. Put some rich soil into a container and plant. Water as the soil dries out. You'll always have a plentiful supply. The little bit of greenery in the window is very pretty, too.

Broiled Halibut
SERVES 4

4 fresh halibut filets
2 teaspoons Kitchen Bouquet
½ cup sweet butter
¼ cup chopped green olives with pimientos
juice of ½ lemon

Line a cookie sheet with parchment and lightly butter the surface. Place the halibut filets close together. With your fingertips, rub with Kitchen Bouquet. Broil for 5 minutes. Turn and rub the other side with the remaining Kitchen Bouquet. Broil for 5 minutes more. Melt butter and add the olives and lemon juice. Spoon the olive sauce over the top of each filet. These are browned and crispy on the outside, tender and juicy on the inside.

While visiting the awe-inspiring Tweedsmuir Provincial Park in west-central British Columbia, Canada, we developed a wonderful friendship with Tom and Judy Martin and their son Chris. They live on beautiful Nimpo Lake, near the park. We were their guests one evening for an outdoor moose steak barbecue, which we will never forget.

As part of the animal herd control program, the provincial government allows limited moose hunting. Tom and Judy wanted us to share their good fortune from a recent hunt and prepared a roaring open fire on the lake's edge. Moose is rarely available to those of us in the midst of civilization, but if it is, here is the best way to enjoy it.

Outdoor Moose Steak

4 steaks of moose
4 tablespoons butter (moose has no fat and the butter must be used)
1 teaspoon dry mustard
½ teaspoon salt
½ teaspoon curry powder

Rub the steaks with butter and seasonings. Let stand for 15 minutes. Sear over an open fire and cook to taste. Serve with a pungent steak sauce. Moose is surprisingly tender but has a very dry texture and a gamey taste, although it is not quite as strong as venison.

Baked Salmon Vancouver

The best-tasting salmon we have ever had was prepared according to this recipe. It's hard to believe that so much fine flavor could result from such simple preparation. The secret, if there is one beyond simplicity, is the freshness of the salmon.

Although salmon is expensive (especially for the freshest), buy a whole fish and serve whatever is left over cold the following day or day after.

Select the fish from your best market source. Line a cookie sheet with parchment cut to twice the size of the sheet, with a bit more for folding.

Rub the fish cavity with ¼ teaspoon salt and ½ teaspoon lemon juice for each pound of fish. Lay on lettuce leaves the size of the fish (this prevents sticking). Rub the top of the fish with melted butter and cover. Let stand for 15 minutes before cooking. Bake in a preheated 375°F. oven for 40 to 60 minutes. It is done when it flakes apart with a fork. Begin testing after 30 minutes of cooking to prevent over-cooking. Serve hot or cold.

Baked Eggs
SERVES 4

8 slices bacon
8 eggs
sea salt and pepper to taste
¼ teaspoon rosemary
8 tablespoons cream
8 tablespoons butter

Grease an 8-section muffin tin with butter. Wrap a strip of bacon around the wall of each section and line the bottom. Break an egg into each lined section and season. Put 1 tablespoon cream and 1 tablespoon butter on top of each. Bake in a preheated 350°F. oven until set, about 30 minutes. Lift out gently with a fork, serving 2 per person. They hold the shape well. Serve with whole-grain bread.

This recipe is from a dear friend. On the day we moved into our new house, she dropped by bringing a beautiful casserole dish with all of the ingredients, in their store packaging, inside. The recipe was thoughtfully tucked inside, too, and a bright bow topped the present. (The water was the only item missing from the gift package.)

Wild Rice Casserole

1 cup wild rice
1 cup grated sharp Cheddar cheese
1 cup diced ripe olives
1 #2 can tomatoes, or 4 medium fresh tomatoes
1 cup small whole mushrooms
½ cup chopped onion
½ cup olive oil
1 teaspoon sea salt
½ teaspoon ground pepper
1½ cups water

Prepare the rice according to package directions. Cook, drain, and chill for several hours. Mix with all the other ingredients and bake in a preheated 325°F. oven for 1½ hours.

This recipe may be made with brown rice or a blend, but the taste will not be quite as delicious. The rice may be cooked a day ahead of time with no change in flavor.

Leftover meats may be added to the casserole or it may be served as is for a meatless meal.

Stuffed Pork Chops
SERVES 4

4 double pork chops
½ cup cooked brown rice
1 slice bacon, crisply cooked
2 tablespoons bread crumbs
1 tablespoon wheat germ
2 tablespoons chopped onion
2 tablespoons chopped celery
⅛ teaspoon poultry seasoning
salt and pepper to taste
1 tablespoon butter or oil
1 cup water

With a very sharp knife carefully slit a pocket in the pork chops, cutting lengthwise almost through to the bone. Mix all stuffing ingredients together and stuff the chops. Sew up the slit with string. Melt a little butter or oil in a heavy skillet. Turn heat up high and quickly brown the chops on both sides, then remove from the fire. Put into the oven, add the water and cover. Bake in a preheated 325°F. oven until tender, about 1 hour. Thicken juices to serve as gravy. Broiled tomatoes are a good accompaniment.

Party Stew Casserole
SERVES 6-8

3 pounds stewing beef, cut into 2-inch cubes

1 cup small green beans

1 cup small green peas

1½ cups tomatoes

1½ cups small white onions

1 cup diced carrots

2 cups beef broth or stock

½ cup white wine

1 bay leaf

4 tablespoons tapioca

1 tablespoon brown sugar

½ cup bread crumbs

Place all of the ingredients in a casserole in the order listed. Cover and bake in a preheated 250°F. oven for 6 to 7 hours. Serve over steamed brown rice.

Robert's Own Shrimp Jacques
SERVES 4

16 large raw shrimp

½ pound butter

4 cloves fresh garlic

⅛ tablespoon chopped parsley

1½ cups coarse cracker crumbs

4 servings cooked wild rice

Wash, peel and devein the shrimp and lay out on paper towels to dry. Melt ¼ pound of butter slowly in two large cast-iron skillets. Thoroughly press 2 cloves of garlic into each skillet. Divide pepper between the two skillets along with the parsley. Butterfly the shrimp and press each side into abundant amounts of cracker crumbs. Heat butter until very near scorching. Quickly put the shrimp in to cook, turning as the underside becomes golden brown. Control heat so as to be very hot without actually burning. Serve immediately, when browned well on both sides, over wild rice. Pour remaining butter directly from the skillet over each plate of shrimp and rice. A good white wine and small salad completes this meal. (Garlic is considered medicinal in many parts of the world.)

Herbs make the difference

Fresh vegetables are naturally best when cooked with very little water or broth until just tender. The worst obscenity to the art of cooking is to use too much water and then discard it, along with a great portion of the vitamins, minerals and natural fresh taste.

Natural herbs can do wonders for all vegetables and many meats, but using them subtly is the answer. Almost all herbs may be bought in the market, but you can never know how old they are. Because the essential oils of these herbs present their flavor, herbs from the grocer's shelf are always suspect. Grow your own! Here are a few that do well in a surprisingly small plot (approximately 3 feet by 3 feet).

Chives: baked potatoes, cheese dishes, omelettes, salads
Lemon thyme: sauces, meats, fish, casseroles. Makes a delicious tea
Oregano: sauces, soups, game meats, mushroom dishes
Parsley: everything from soup to decorative accents
Rosemary: meats, eggs, fish, vegetables, herb butter
Shallots: sauces
Sweet basil: salads, tomatoes, eggs, meat, spaghetti sauces, relish
Tarragon: salad dressings, chicken, steeped in vinegar, fish
Winter savory: meat stuffings, sauces, soups, stews

I have found winter savory and oregano the most difficult to grow with success. Perhaps your soil, together with a green thumb, will find them easier.

Seasoned Herb Salt

6 tablespoons salt

2 tablespoons paprika

1 teaspoon dry mustard

½ teaspoon dried parsley leaves

½ teaspoon dried lemon thyme leaves

½ teaspoon dried marjoram

½ teaspoon garlic salt

½ teaspoon celery salt

¼ teaspoon curry powder

¼ teaspoon onion powder

⅛ teaspoon dill seed

Put everything into the blender on low speed until mixed well. You may also use a small mortar and pestle. It will take a bit longer but blends well.

Be sure to use this herb salt for any dish you find appropriate. Don't over-use, the subtle taste is most desirable.

Many people don't have a particular fondness for turnips, but this tasty dish has converted some of the most entrenched turnip haters.

Glazed Turnips

4 medium white turnips

½ teaspoon salt

1 cup water (approximate)

2 to 4 tablespoons sweet butter

¼ cup molasses

salt and pepper to taste

Wash, peel and quarter the turnips. Cook in a saucepan with salt and water over medium heat for about 20 minutes, or until tender. Drain and mash. Add butter and molasses, mixing thoroughly. Put in a baking dish with salt and pepper to taste. Bake in a preheated 350°F. oven for 10 minutes.

Never-Fail Spinach Soufflé

1¼ cups cooked spinach

2 eggs, separated

1 cup milk

⅔ cup stone-ground wheat cracker crumbs

2 tablespoons minced onion

1 small clove garlic

salt and pepper to taste

¼ cup butter

Cook the spinach and drain well. Chop. Mix egg yolks with the milk and the cooled spinach. Add the cracker crumbs, onion, garlic (put through press), salt and pepper. Melt the butter and cool slightly. Add half of the melted butter to the spinach mixture, stirring well. Beat the egg whites until stiff, then fold in gently. Pour the rest of the melted butter into a casserole dish. Add the spinach mixture. Place the casserole into a shallow pan of water in a 350°F. oven for 35 to 40 minutes until it is well set. There are not many calories here, but lots of flavor and good natural nutrition.

Stuffed Carrots

8 to 12 carrots

2 tablespoons cracker crumbs

1 teaspoon sesame seeds

1 egg

¼ teaspoon paprika

¼ teaspoon salt

1 tablespoon butter

½ teaspoon parsley, chopped

Cook carrots whole. When tender, cool and cut in half, lengthwise. Remove the dark core to make a shallow furrow the length of the carrot. Mash the removed carrot in a bowl. Blend with the rest of the ingredients except for the butter and parsley. Fill the cavity of the carrots and dot with butter. Sprinkle the parsley on top. Bake at 350°F. for 10 minutes. This is a good change of pace and a delightful persuasion to a family member who needs coaxing toward this nutritious tuber.

Fried Beans and Corn, Cream-style

1½ cups green beans, cut into 1-inch pieces
2 ears fresh corn
2 tablespoons butter
¼ cup cream
sea salt and pepper to taste

Cook the green beans, saving the cooking water. Cut the corn from the cob. Scrape the cob with the blade of the kitchen knife (this was called "milking the cob" by good cooks in the South). Melt the butter in a skillet. Add the corn, corn milk, cream, salt and pepper. Cook over medium heat until corn is tender, 2 or 3 minutes. Add the green beans and continue cooking to reduce liquid. Serve piping hot.

Broiled Tomatoes
SERVES 4

4 firm ripe tomatoes, halved
2 tablespoons grated Parmesan cheese
1 tablespoon wheat germ
¼ teaspoon oregano (or herb seasoning of your choice)

Put the tomatoes into a baking dish. Sprinkle the cheese, wheat germ and seasoning on top. Run under the broiler until very hot and crunchy on top about 3 to 5 minutes.

Sweet Potato-Orange Casserole
SERVES 4

3 medium sweet potatoes, baked until tender
½ cup freshly squeezed orange juice (with pulp)
¼ cup honey
¼ cup sweet butter
¼ cup chopped pecans

Mash the sweet potatoes. Add the other ingredients and blend until creamy. Bake in a lightly buttered baking dish at 325°F. for 20 minutes.

Garden Zucchini

8 fresh zucchini, about 4 inches in length
½ teaspoon garlic salt
1 tablespoon sweet butter

Wash the zucchini, remove ends and cut in half lengthwise. Lay in single layers on the trivet of your pressure cooker or in a steamer.

Sprinkle with garlic salt and add about ¼ cup water. Cover and steam until just tender, 8 to 10 minutes. Top with butter on a decorative plate.

This delightful rice is party-pretty, family-pleasing, and so very, very easy.

Pink Rice

1 cup brown rice
¼ teaspoon garlic powder
¼ teaspoon paprika
½ cup butter
1 11-ounce can consommé Madrilène

Butter a casserole dish (a glass one is good because of the pretty pink color of the rice). Pour in the uncooked rice and seasonings. Put the butter in the middle and pour the consommé over all. Bake, covered, in a preheated 325°F. oven for 1 hour.

Fried Squash Blossoms

You can also use pumpkin blossoms for this unusual treat. Since most of us don't usually have many of these blossoms, it's a good idea to ask a farmer for them when on an outing into the country. Many blossoms do not produce fruit, and there's no harm done by collecting as many of these as time and the source will allow. Wash and remove the stamen. Roll lightly in flour, slightly beaten egg and cracker crumbs in that order. Fry in 1 inch of oil (not deep-fried)—safflower or sesame oil is best. Cook until brown, turning once. Drain and enjoy before or as a part of any meal. They are really worth the effort. Pumpkin blossoms taste more like shrimp than pumpkin.

Fourth of July New Potatoes and Peas

8 to 12 whole new potatoes
1 pound peas in the shell
½ cup cream
1 teaspoon Seasoned Herb salt
¼ teaspoon lemon pepper
1 small mint leaf, slightly crushed

This recipe is designed to get you out of doors and into the sun for a quiet contemplation of the world about you. Sit under a tree if you must, but do shell the peas outside. Peel the potatoes out there too. Cook both separately. Put the cream in a baking dish. Add the salt, lemon pepper and mint leaf. Put in the potatoes and peas. Combine lightly and bake for about 30 minutes in a 325°F. oven.

If you are fortunate enough to have a small garden spot and grow these potatoes and peas yourself, this is an even more pleasurable dish.

Are you beginning to get the idea that the simplest, most natural foods are in fact the best? It's sometimes odd to us that many people seem to complicate things on purpose.

Fried Bean Sprouts

4 tablespoons peanut oil

1 pound fresh Homemade bean sprouts

1 clove garlic

2 tablespoons soy sauce

1 teaspoon arrowroot flour

½ teaspoon ground ginger

¼ teaspoon sea salt

3 slices bacon, crisp fried, drained and crumbled

1 tablespoon minced green onion

Heat the oil in a skillet or wok. Add the bean sprouts and garlic. Stir constantly over high heat for about 5 minutes until sprouts begin to brown. Mix the soy sauce, arrowroot, ginger and salt together and add to sprouts. Reduce the heat to low and cook for about 2 minutes longer, stirring constantly as it thickens. Put into a warm serving dish and sprinkle with the crumbled bacon and minced green onion.

One of the secrets of this dish is long simmering to enrich the flavor. This recipe has been in our family for many years and finding the nail in our serving meant that we would have strength for the coming year. Likewise, finding the dime meant riches. It's still a lot of fun to play that game on the first day of a new year.

New Year's Day Black-eyed Peas

½ pound slab bacon or ham hock
1½ cups dried black-eyed peas
1 quart water
1 teaspoon sea salt
¼ teaspoon pepper
1 nail
1 dime

Have the butcher crack the bone of the ham hock (try to get one with extra meat attached). Soak the peas overnight in water to cover. Boil the bacon or ham hock in water for about 1 hour. Skim excess grease off the top and cut up meat, returning it to the stock. Drain the peas and add to the stock. Simmer slowly until the peas are tender. The stock should have a rich caramel color. Add the nail and the dime with the seasonings.

This is a favorite from the German side of our family.

Kraut Relish
MAKES 4 CUPS

1 cup raw sugar
½ cup vinegar
1 quart jar sauerkraut
2 cups finely chopped celery
1 2-ounce jar pimentos, chopped fine
1 large onion, chopped fine
1 teaspoon sea salt
½ teaspoon pepper

Heat the sugar and vinegar until the sugar dissolves. Cool to lukewarm. Drain the sauerkraut and combine with all vegetables and seasonings. Put into a large wide-mouthed jar or crock and pour the vinegar-sugar mixture over all. Mix well and chill in the refrigerator. This relish keeps very well in the refrigerator for 3 to 4 weeks.

This recipe is from a friend who grew up in Boston. The flavor is as good as any we have experienced—anywhere.

Boston	1½ cups tiny navy beans (dried)
Baked	¼ pound salt pork, finely diced
Beans	½ cup minced onion
	¼ cup sorghum
	¼ cup catsup
	1 tablespoon mustard
	1 teaspoon sea salt
	¼ teaspoon cayenne pepper

Soak the beans overnight in water to cover. Drain and add enough fresh cold water to cover again. Simmer slowly with the salt pork for 2 hours, or until the skins loosen when you take some up on a spoon and blow on them. Drain off cooking water, cover with very cold water, then quickly drain again.

Mix with all other ingredients. Put into a covered baking dish or pottery crock. Cook in a preheated 250°F. oven for about 8 hours. If the beans dry out too much add a bit of water or soup stock. Individual bean pots are fun, but so is the practice of letting everyone ladle out their own.

This is a great all-vegetable meal in itself.

Stuffed	4 medium green peppers
Green	½ cup chopped celery
Peppers	½ cup blanched almonds
SERVES 4	½ cup sliced mushrooms
	2 tablespoons butter
	2 tablespoons unbleached flour
	½ cup chicken stock
	½ cup cream
	1 teaspoon chopped parsley
	⅛ teaspoon lemon thyme
	¼ cup grated sharp Cheddar cheese
	1 tablespoon bread crumbs

Wash the peppers, cut off tops and clean out seeds. Place in a buttered oven-proof dish so that the sides of the peppers are touching. Parboil the celery until just tender. Drain and add the almonds and mushrooms. Set aside. Make a cream sauce: melt the butter, stir in the flour until smooth, and add the stock, cream and seasonings. Stir over medium heat until thickened. Add the vegetables. Stuff the pepper cavities with the mixture and sprinkle grated cheese and bread crumbs over the top. Add enough water to come up about ½ inch on the peppers. Cover with foil and bake for 30 minutes in a preheated 350°F. oven, or until peppers are tender to the tines of a fork.

"Gram," as her friends call her, makes a yearly trek to England. She is simply the most vivacious, active, energetic 80-year-old we know. She inspired this one.

London Vegetarian Casserole

½ cup wheat germ

4 small carrots, grated

1½ cups green beans, cooked and cut into small pieces

herb salt and white pepper to taste

4 tablespoons butter

½ pound grated cheese

Butter a shallow casserole dish. Line with wheat germ. Spread grated carrots over this. Add the green beans with ½ cup of their cooking liquid. Season and dot with butter, then top with grated cheese. Bake for about 20 minutes at 350°F. The cheese should have thoroughly melted and be bubbly.

Breads

Baking flours vary in gluten content and are subject to many variables during the baking process. For health's sake, we prefer unbleached, whole-wheat, rye and cracked grains. Commercial sandwich breads are generally so filled with air, and ingredients that serve the profit motive of the baker, we rarely have them in the house. The more bread you bake, the easier it becomes.

This wonderful-tasting, nutritious burger bun was inspired by Robert who insisted it would be perfect for hamburgers.

Cracked-wheat Honey Buns
12 BUNS

1 package yeast or 1 tablespoon dry yeast granules

¼ cup warm water

1 cup milk

2 tablespoons butter

¼ cup honey

1 teaspoon salt

3 cups whole-wheat flour

1 cup cracked wheat grains

1 cup unbleached white flour

2 tablespoons sesame seeds

2 tablespoons cracked wheat

1 egg, slightly beaten

¼ cup melted butter

Dissolve the yeast in warm water. Heat the milk, 2 tablespoons butter, honey and salt until dissolved. Cool to lukewarm. Add to yeast mixture. Add 2 cups whole-wheat flour and 1 cup cracked wheat. Beat with an electric mixer for about 2 minutes. Add the unbleached flour, mixing well with a wooden spoon. Begin adding the last cup of whole-wheat flour until the dough handles easily (we usually find that ⅓ cup is enough). Use the remaining whole-wheat flour on the bread board as needed for kneading. Push the dough with the heels of your hand, folding the ends over and kneading away from you with a firm action. Do this until the dough is elastic but resists a bit. Warm a bowl and butter lightly. Invert the mound of dough and cover, buttered side up. Let rise in a warm place. (We use the oven with a dish of hot water, changing the water as it cools.) When the bread is doubled in bulk, turn onto the floured bread board and knead as before. Return to the oven and let rise again. When doubled in bulk, turn out onto the board and roll out to a ½-inch thickness. Cut out a dozen buns, using a coffee can as the cutter.

Lightly grease a large cookie sheet with butter and sprinkle the sesame seed and 2 tablespoons cracked wheat evenly over the surface, saving back about half for topping off the buns. Brush the tops with beaten egg and sprinkle on seeds and cracked grains. The buns should be touching on the baking sheet. Let rise 20 to 30 minutes, covered. When about doubled in bulk, bake in a preheated 400°F. oven for 15 to 20 minutes, allowing the tops to be well-browned. When done, remove from the oven, cool a bit, then put into several plastic bags or covered container.

These buns are very good and have extraordinary amounts of good whole-grain nutrition. They should become a favorite at your house.

This recipe is from friends in British Columbia, Canada, where we are assured that women bake bread to offset the dreary cold winter days.

Braided Egg Bread
MAKES 2 LOAVES

1 package yeast or 1 tablespoon dry yeast granules

½ cup warm water

2 tablespoons raw sugar

1½ cups warm milk

½ cup raw sugar

1 tablespoon salt

¼ cup soft butter or vegetable shortening

4 to 6 cups unbleached white flour

4 eggs

Dissolve the yeast in warm water with 2 tablespoons sugar. When it begins to rise and bubble (about 10 minutes) add the milk, ½ cup sugar

and salt. Add the softened butter and 2 cups flour. Beat vigorously or use an electric mixer. Add 3 eggs and beat again. Using a wooden spoon, stir in the remaining flour until it handles easily. Use only enough flour for a good elastic dough. Knead on pastry cloth or board, then put in a warm place to rise to double bulk. Do this twice.

Punch down and divide into sixths. Roll out six long strands with your hands, stretching as you go. Put three ends together and braid. Make both braided loaves and brush generously with the remaining egg which has been slightly beaten. Let rise again on greased cookie sheets and bake in a preheated 400°F. oven for 20 or 25 minutes.

No-knead English Muffins

½ cup hot milk

¼ cup polyunsaturated shortening

1½ teaspoons sea salt

1 tablespoon raw sugar

½ cup cold water

1 package yeast or 1 tablespoon dry yeast granules

3 cups sifted unbleached flour

2 to 4 tablespoons cornmeal

Combine the hot milk, shortening, salt and sugar. When the shortening has melted, cool to lukewarm by adding the cold water. Crumble the yeast into the mixture and blend. Sift the flour and add, stirring until well blended. Cover and let stand for 15 minutes. Roll out to ¼-inch thickness. For small muffins use a regular biscuit cutter, for larger ones use a coffee can. Sprinkle cornmeal on several cookie sheets. Lay rounds of dough on this and sprinkle with more cornmeal.

Let rise until doubled in bulk, about 1 hour. Bake slowly on an ungreased griddle set at 300°F. Cooking time is 6 or 7 minutes per side. When setting the rounds on the griddle, be gentle so they won't fall. When turning they will deflate and fall a bit, but don't worry about it. If you don't have a controlled-heat griddle, use an ungreased skillet set on a low flame. If, cooking this way, you find the muffins cooking faster than the prescribed time, reduce the flame. Do not try to bake in the oven. When cool store in plastic bags. To serve, split and toast, topped with sweet butter.

Old-fashioned Oatmeal Bread

4½ to 5 cups unbleached flour
¼ cup sugar
1½ cups uncooked oats
1½ teaspoons sea salt
2 packages yeast or 2 tablespoons dry yeast granules
1 cup milk
⅓ cup butter
½ cup cold water
2 eggs
melted butter

In a large bowl mix well 1½ cups flour and the sugar, oats, salt and yeast. In a saucepan heat the milk until warm. Add the butter and stir until it melts. Add cold water. When lukewarm, gradually add to dry ingredients and beat 2 minutes by hand or on medium speed in an electric mixer. Add the eggs and 1 more cup flour. Beat again until blended. Work in the remaining flour. Cover and let rise until doubled in bulk, about 1 hour. Punch down and beat vigorously for 1 minute. Turn into greased loaf pans and allow to rise. Bake in a preheated 375°F. oven for 40 or 50 minutes. The loaves should come out of the pan easily when the sides are tapped. Brush tops with melted butter and cool on wire racks.

Grit Cakes for Breakfast

½ cup hominy grits
2 cups water
salt and pepper to taste
¼ cup butter
½ cup diced Cheddar cheese
1 egg
¼ cup milk

Cook the grits in water with salt and pepper. Stir constantly, preparing according to package directions. When cooked add the butter and cheese, stirring until the cheese is melted. Remove from the fire. Beat the egg slightly and add the milk. Blend the mixture into the grits. Press into a buttered casserole dish and bake in a preheated 325°F. oven for 35 or 40 minutes. Cut into squares and serve with scrambled eggs. Serve with sweet butter and honey-berry syrup (see below).

Substitute this tasty dish for potatoes or rice.

Good Spoon Bread

2 cups water
1 teaspoon sea salt
1 cup cornmeal
2 tablespoons butter
3 eggs
½ cup milk

Bring the water to a boil, add the salt and cornmeal. Cook for about 5 minutes. Remove from the fire and add the butter. Beat the eggs until fluffy. Stir in the milk and add to the meal mixture. Bake in a lightly greased casserole dish at 375°F. for 45 or 50 minutes. Spoon out to serve.

Honey-berry Syrup

Slightly warm 1 cup honey in the top of a double boiler. Slowly add ⅛ to ¼ cup of your favorite organic juice concentrate, stirring to combine. Pour into honey dispenser and use over grit cakes, pancakes or waffles. Absolutely delicious and nutritious too. Cranberry, apricot, boysenberry, strawberry and raspberry juice concentrates are our favorites. Be sure the juices are organic—it's healthier!

The dough for this recipe can be made in advance and stored in the refrigerator.

Banana Nut Bread or Muffins

⅔ cup raw sugar
½ cup butter
2 eggs
2 cups unbleached flour
1 teaspoon baking powder
1 teaspoon sea salt
3 ripe bananas, mashed
⅔ cup chopped pecans

Cream the sugar and butter. Beat in the eggs. Combine the flour, baking powder and salt and sift. Add to the egg mixture along with the mashed bananas. The dough will be slightly stiff. Add the nuts last. Chill for at least 1 hour. Whether making bread loaves or muffins, lightly butter the pan or tin, fill to two-thirds full and bake in a preheated 375°F. oven for 15 or 20 minutes.

Variation   Raisins may be added to the dough with the nuts.

Gooseberry Bread

1 egg

½ cup raw sugar

2 tablespoons butter

1 cup gooseberry jam

3 teaspoons baking powder

2 cups unbleached flour

½ teaspoon sea salt

½ cup milk

Beat the egg and add the sugar. Melt the butter and add. Add the jam and mix well. Sift the flour with other dry ingredients and add alternately with the milk to the creamed mixture. Grease 5 x 9-inch loaf pan and bake in a preheated 350°F. oven for about 1 hour. Check after 45 minutes. The bread is done when a toothpick comes out clean.

Alberta, Canada, still abounds in wildlife. There are numerous guest lodges throughout the province that offer everything from skiing to nature hikes. One such lodge is a favorite haunt of ours for just getting out into open country in the company of an experienced trail guide. One of the best trail foods developed by our friend Charlie is this granola.

Granola

3 pounds rolled oats

2 cups shredded coconut

2 cups nuts and seeds (sunflower, cashews, almonds)

2 cups wheat germ

1 tablespoon sea salt

1½ cups safflower oil

⅔ cup water

3 tablespoons vanilla extract

1½ cups honey

1 to 2 cups raisins or dried fruits

Blend the dry ingredients together in a large bowl. Set aside. In another bowl combine the oil, water, vanilla and honey. Beat together with a wire whisk. Pour over the dry ingredients and mix well with your hands until everything is thoroughly blended. Spread the mixture out about ½ inch thick on a lightly greased cookie sheet. Place in a slow oven (250°F.) for 1 to 1½ hours. Turn mixture every half hour until oats are golden brown. Remove from the oven and turn once more. Cool. Add the raisins and other dried fruits. Store in a cool place, tightly covered. For hikes put individual portions in small plastic bags, or have readily available at home for nutritious snacks.

This does seem like a lot of bother for something that can be bought already prepared, but the flavor and satisfaction of making it in your own kitchen will certainly compensate for the trouble.

Homemade Noodles

2 eggs

2 or 3 tablespoons water (4 half eggshells full)

1½ to 1⅔ cups unbleached or whole-wheat flour
   (depending on the size of the eggs used)

½ teaspoon sea salt

Beat the eggs and water with a wire whisk. Combine the flour and salt and add to egg mixture, a little at a time. When the resulting dough begins to pull away from the sides of the bowl, turn onto a floured board or cloth and knead until just smooth. Do this gently, not roughly as in kneading bread dough, as overkneading or overmixing will toughen the noodles. Roll out into a very thin sheet, then roll up the sheet into a long roll and cut across the roll into ¼- to ½-inch strips. Drop the noodles gently into simmering broth or salted water and cook until tender and fluffy, about 8 or 10 minutes. These noodles will keep well for several hours before cooking if you wish to make them up ahead of time.

Beverages

This is particularly good on a cold winter's afternoon along with home baked nut bread or **Granola cookies.** *It is equally good when allowed to cool and poured over ice cubes in summer. The spicy taste gives it real character.*

Hot
Apple
Cider
ABOUT 3½ QUARTS

2 quarts organic apple juice
1½ quarts organic cranberry juice
4 sticks cinnamon
4 whole cloves
¼ cup brown sugar or honey

Put everything into a large pan or coffeepot, bring to a boil, and cook until very hot. Remove from the fire and let stand for about 5 minutes before serving.

Milk
Shakes

1 cup milk
½ cup Freezer ice cream
flavored whipped cream

Blend the milk and ice cream in a blender or with a rotary beater until thick and frothy and top with whipped cream.

Variations   Using the above basic milk recipe, add a variety of flavorings such as:

organic juice concentrates
mashed bananas
fresh berries
honey carob

Or leave out the milk and add sparkling soda water to the glass a little at a time.

Ginger Yogurt

1 cup fresh Yogurt

2 tablespoons honey

⅛ teaspoon ground ginger

Put in the blender with 4 to 6 ice cubes. Blend until frothy, fluffy and icy cold. Very cool to look at as well as to drink. A nutritious pick-me-up.

Use the best available. These little jewels are chock full of vitamin C.

Rose-hip Tea

4 teaspoons dried rose hips

1 quart boiling water

4 tablespoons honey

Put the rose hips into a teapot. Pour in the boiling water and let steep for 5 to 10 minutes. Add honey and serve in warmed cups or mugs.

While traveling in the rugged interior of northern Canada in a motor home we met a young American couple, who were trying to begin a new life in the wild out-of-doors. They were quite determined to make a success of this new venture. To support themselves through the hard winter, they cut firewood, selling cord after cord to the scattered residents. Their hardy five-year-old son worked with them every day after school. The wife had developed a magnificent home remedy to ward off colds. She gathered the abundant rose hips of the area and dried them in the house during good weather. At the beginning of winter she produced this marvelous syrup.

Rose-hip Syrup

2 pounds rose hips

1 quart water

½ to 1 cup honey

Boil all together and strain. Bottle and set on the shelf. A teaspoon a day for each gave them a good source of vitamin C and the vigor to cut the firewood.

Strawberry Tea

2 large handfuls strawberry leaves, washed and crushed

1 quart water

honey

Put leaves in a pot and pour boiling water over them. Steep for 10 minutes and sweeten with honey.

Breakfast Drink

1 cup milk
1 egg
1 tablespoon wheat germ
½ cup orange juice
½ banana
cinnamon for topping

Blend in a blender until thick and creamy. Top with a dash of cinnamon.

One-Two-Three-Punch

1 quart organic apricot nectar
2 quarts organic grape juice
3 quarts lemonade
honey (optional)

Mix and add honey for extra sweetness. Chill by floating a large chunk of ice in the center of a punch bowl. Garnish with fresh mint leaves.

Russian Tea
MAKES 1 GALLON

3 oranges
4 lemons
3½ quarts cold water
2 cups honey
2½ cups water
2 sticks cinnamon
1 tablespoon whole cloves
½ cup tea leaves

Squeeze the oranges and lemons. Set the juice aside. Put the fruit halves into the 3½ quarts cold water. Bring to a boil and strain. Set aside. Add the honey to 2½ cups water and boil for 5 minutes. Add the cinnamon sticks and cloves. Boil for another 3 minutes. Add the tea leaves and continue boiling for another 3 minutes. Strain this into the orange-lemon water. Stir all liquid and let stand overnight to develop full flavor. Serve hot or cold.

The evils of "demon rum" are or should be well known to most of us. However, there are notable exceptions with regard to the use of alcohol to consider. Namely, a lively old family friend who died at the age of 86. Sam drank a straight shot of bourbon every morning of his life from age 16 onward and another upon retiring at night. When asked why he drank the whiskey in the morning, he laughed and said, "that's to get my heart started!"

Why the drink at night? "Oh that one's to signal my heart to take it easy for the next eight hours."

As far as we know that amount of alcohol was all he ever indulged in, with one exception. He had two mint juleps in the mid-afternoon of every June 21st. That, he said, "was to celebrate the first day of summer."

Mint Julep

half a lemon

1 teaspoon confectioner's sugar for each julep

2 sprigs of fresh mint for each julep

finely crushed ice

2 ounces aged bourbon whiskey for each julep

Frost a glass by running a half lemon around the top of a very cold glass. Roll the top in confectioner's sugar and set into the freezer. When ready to serve, crush the mint leaves in the bottom of the glass and dust in a bit of confectioner's sugar. Fill with crushed ice. Pour in the bourbon (it should come to within an inch of the top). Stick mint leaves into the top and dust lightly with confectioner's sugar. Serve as is or with a straw.

A final thought on beverages

Good herb teas have become a favorite around our house, not just for their general medicinal qualities but because of our acquired taste for them. Everyone has a favorite. Select those you enjoy most and have them often.

Desserts

We generally agree that desserts should be light, nutritious and good tasting, but not overburdened with sugar. The ones included here meet that requirement as far as we are concerned.

Boiled Custard

4 eggs
1 cup honey
4 cups milk
1 teaspoon vanilla extract
whipped cream
nutmeg

Beat the eggs until light. Add the honey and beat again. Warm the milk in the top of a double boiler. Add the egg mixture gradually and stir constantly. Continue cooking, stirring occasionally until the custard coats a silver spoon, about 10 or 15 minutes. Remove from the fire and add the vanilla. Chill and serve in individual custard cups topped with a dollop of whipped cream and a dash of nutmeg. Overcooking this custard will cause it to curdle, so be very careful. If it should curdle, strain through a strainer or put into the blender on low speed until just blended.

Persimmon Loaf

1 cup flour
3 teaspoons baking powder
½ teaspoon sea salt
1 cup raw sugar
1 cup persimmon pulp
½ cup soft bread crumbs
1 cup dates
1 cup chopped walnuts
1 teaspoon vanilla extract

Mix first 5 ingredients together. Mix last 4 ingredients together and blend. Grease and flour a loaf pan. Bake 1 hour at 350°F. Serve warm with whipped cream or cold in thin slices.

Shortly after we were married, my husband casually commented that one of his favorite desserts was prune whip. So I found a recipe, a fairly complicated one that was baked in a water bath.

That evening I proudly served it. My husband stared at the plate and said, "What's that?" "That's the prune whip you asked for," I pleaded. "That's not it," he said. After a frantic phone call to his mother I got the recipe for his "real" prune whip. Try it. This is light, flavorful and nutritious.

Prune
Whip

1 cup cooked and mashed prunes

2 cups whipped cream with a bit of honey and vanilla

Blend and put into parfait glasses. Chill thoroughly.

Buttermilk
Sherbet

1 tablespoon unflavored gelatin

¼ cup water

1 cup raw sugar

¼ teaspoon sea salt

2 cups fresh buttermilk

1 cup fresh fruit, crushed (pineapple, strawberries, raspberries)

2 tablespoons lemon juice

Soften gelatin in water. Stir the sugar, salt and buttermilk together until the sugar is dissolved. Blend together and add the fruit and lemon juice. Turn into an ice cream freezer or put into freezer section of refrigerator, stirring every 10 minutes until frozen.

Icebox
Gingerbread

½ cup butter

½ cup raw sugar

2 eggs

½ cup molasses

½ cup milk

1 teaspoon vinegar

2 cups unbleached flour

1 teaspoon baking powder

¼ teaspoon nutmeg

¼ teaspoon cinnamon

¼ teaspoon allspice

¼ cup nuts

½ cup raisins

Cream the butter and sugar. Add the eggs one at a time. Add molasses. Mix the vinegar with milk (to force sour). Blend the dry ingredients and add alternately with milk/vinegar mixture, ⅓ at a time. Add nuts and raisins before the last ⅓ of flour-milk mixture is added. Store in refrigerator. Bake as needed in a preheated 350°F. oven for 15 to 20 minutes. Flavor whipped cream with cinnamon as a topping or softened cream cheese blended with yogurt, honey and a bit of lemon juice.

Freezer
Ice cream

1 quart milk

1 quart raw cream

or

2 quarts milk (for less-rich version)

4 whole eggs

1½ cups honey

¼ teaspoon salt

1 tablespoon vanilla

Heat the milk and cream until it begins to bubble. Set aside. Beat the eggs and honey until lemon colored and light. Add the slightly cooled milk, salt and vanilla, stirring constantly. Turn in an ice cream freezer.

Serve this delicious ice cream with fresh fruit in season or honey-flavored fruit syrup.

Cream-
cheese
Soufflé

1 6-ounce package cream cheese

¾ cup sour cream

2 tablespoons honey

¼ teaspoon sea salt

3 eggs, separated

whipped cream and strawberries or raspberries

Soften the cream cheese, add the sour cream and beat until smooth. Stir in the honey and salt. Beat the egg yolks until light and add. Beat whites until stiff and fold into batter. Pour into lightly greased baking dish and bake at 325°F. for 30-35 minutes. Serve immediately with whipped cream and fresh berries.

A delightful holiday dessert or nutritious afternoon snack.

Stuffed
Dates

1 tablespoon butter

½ pound pecan halves

½ teaspoon sea salt

½ pound dried dates

¼ cup raw sugar

Melt the butter and toss with pecans being careful not to break them. Lay on a cookie sheet, sprinkle with salt and bake in a preheated 350°F. oven for 5 to 10 minutes until browned slightly, turning once. Cool.

Split each date open and remove seed. Replace with a toasted pecan half. Roll in the sugar.

Our cousin Margaret developed this recipe many years ago when she had only a wood stove for cooking. There was no temperature control of any kind, and it was difficult for anyone but herself to know just how long to cook anything.

Wood-stove Pumpkin Pie

GOOD BASIC PIE CRUST
½ cup vegetable shortening
¼ cup boiling water
1⅓ cups unbleached flour
¼ teaspoon sea salt
¼ teaspoon baking powder
¼ cup chopped or slivered almonds

PUMPKIN FILLING
2 eggs, separated
1 cup stewed and drained pumpkin
½ cup raw sugar
1 tablespoon sweet butter, melted
¼ teaspoon sea salt
¼ teaspoon nutmeg
½ teaspoon cinnamon
½ cup milk

Cream the shortening with the boiling water. Blend the flour, salt and baking powder and add. Stir until the mixture forms a ball. Chill in the refrigerator for 1 hour. Roll out thin and line a 10-inch pie pan, shaping the edges. Press the almonds firmly into the crust. Set into the refrigerator to chill thoroughly. This pie crust is fine with any filling.

Beat the egg yolks slightly. Add the pumpkin, sugar, butter and spices. Beat for 1 minute. Beat the egg whites until stiff and fold into the mixture. Add the milk and stir gently. Pour into the unbaked pie shell and bake for 10 minutes in a preheated 400°F. oven. Lower the oven temperature to 325°F. and continue baking until set, about 25 or 30 minutes. When a silver knife blade comes out clean, it is done. Serve as is or with whipped raw cream, slightly sweetened with honey.

This is delicious for breakfast, brunch, or an evening dessert.

Fresh Cranberry Coffee Cake

½ cup shortening
1 cup raw sugar
1 egg
2 cups sifted unbleached flour
2 teaspoons baking powder
¼ teaspoon sea salt
¾ cup milk
½ teaspoon vanilla extract
1 cup fresh cranberries, halved
confectioner's sugar

Cream the shortening and sugar. Add the egg. Sift the dry ingredients and add alternately with milk and vanilla. Fold in the cranberry halves. Bake in a greased square baking pan at 350°F. for 45 or 50 minutes. Dust lightly with confectioner's sugar and serve warm with whipped sweet butter.

This was served to us on china decorated with apples on Apple Lane at Apple Hill outside Placerville, California.

Harvest Apple Cake

1½ cups vegetable shortening
2 eggs
2 cups raw sugar
3 cups unbleached flour
1 teaspoon baking powder
1 teaspoon sea salt
1 teaspoon cinnamon
2 teaspoons vanilla extract
½ cup chopped nuts
4 cups harvest-time apples, diced with a bit of peel left on

Beat the shortening, eggs and sugar in a mixer until well blended. Add the dry ingredients, vanilla, nuts and apples, folding in with a wooden spoon. Bake in a greased and floured 13 x 9 inch cake pan in a preheated 350°F. oven for about 1 hour. Serve plain or with a bit of whipped cream or ice cream.

Carrot Cake with Whipped Cream Icing

1 cup raw sugar

1 cup polyunsaturated oil

3 eggs

1 teaspoon sea salt

1⅓ cups unbleached flour

2½ teaspoons baking powder

1½ teaspoons cinnamon

2 cups chopped carrots

½ cup chopped nuts

½ cup raisins

¾ cup brown sugar

2 cups whipping cream

Beat the sugar and oil together with a mixer. Add the egss, one at a time. Beat well. Sift the dry ingredients together and add. Gently fold in the carrots, nuts and raisins. Bake in greased and floured cake pans in two or three layers (whichever you prefer) for 1 hour at 300°F. Cool before frosting. Put the brown sugar and whipping cream in a bowl, then set into the refrigerator for about 1 hour to get very cold. When thoroughly chilled whip until stiff and spreadable. Frost between layers, on sides and top. Store in the refrigerator until serving time.

Granola Cookies

1 cup melted butter

1 cup raw sugar

1 cup brown sugar

2 eggs

2 cups unbleached flour

1 teaspoon sea salt

2 teaspoons baking powder

3½ cups Granola

1 teaspoon vanilla

½ cup coconut

Mix the butter and sugars. Beat the eggs slightly and add. Sift together the flour, salt and baking powder and add. Add the granola, vanilla and coconut. (It may take a bit of doing to get everything thoroughly blended, but it will happen.)

Drop the dough by the spoonful onto a greased cookie sheet. During baking they spread out nicely for a round cookie 3½ to 4 inches in diameter.

Bake 8 or 10 minutes in a preheated 350°F. oven. The longer they bake, the crispier they will be. Store in a tightly-closed container. One quarter of an apple in the cookie jar will help keep them soft and chewy.

A delicious after-dinner drink.

Carob Hot Chocolate

4 cups milk

8 tablespoons carob powder

4 tablespoons brown sugar

2 tablespoons honey

½ cup heavy cream (optional)

¼ teaspoon cinnamon

Beat the milk, carob powder, sugar and honey with a rotary beater or blender until everything is smooth. Heat to piping hot. Whipped cream (if desired) and cinnamon tops off this delight. Have big mugs to hold the heat. Sit around the fireplace and talk to each other about whatever seems to be important about your lives together. Food is a remarkable therapy when blended well with concern for one another.

Where to Buy It

Abalone Most fresh fish markets. Some markets will special order.

Aduki beans Most health food stores.

Aebleskiver pan May be found in gourmet sections of most department stores.

Automatic rice warmer May be found in many Japanese markets and specialty shops.

Bamboo skewers Food market gourmet sections or Japanese markets.

Bonita Bonita is considered a game fish and not available in many states fresh. Gourmet sections of food markets and fish markets will usually carry dried, flake form.

Cast-iron skillet Most department and hardware stores carry these. Look for well-seasoned varieties in junk shops (often a bargain).

Cheeses Most food markets and health food stores have good varieties. A good source of information on various cheeses and sources is Fisher Cheese Company, Wapakoneta, Ohio 45895. For Danish Cheeses: Ecko Denmark, Hammerichsgade 2, Copenhagen, Denmark.

Chervil Health food stores or gourmet department of most food markets. Seeds are at garden supply places.

Chopsticks Oriental food markets and department stores. A restaurant in your area will usually be glad to give you a source.

Cilantro Found in most food markets (also ask for "Chinese parsley").

Cloudberries Available in a variety of gourmet sections. If unavailable locally, may be ordered directly from Jurgensen's Markets, 601 South Lake, Pasadena, California 91101.

Eel Most fresh fish markets, specialty delicatessens or Oriental food markets.

Ginger root Available at many food markets, specialty shops and Oriental food markets.

Gooseberries Available canned at many food markets.

Herring Baltic herring (also Nova Scotia herring) available in several forms at many fresh fish markets.

Horseradish, green Most large food markets. Also in powdered form.

Kelp, dried   Available in packages at most fresh fish markets, gourmet shops and health food stores.

Kelp, fresh   Rarely available but occasionally found in Japanese or fresh fish markets.

Kelp, ground   Health food stores.

Lingonberries   Canned berries may be found in many specialty sections or may be ordered directly from Jurgensen's Markets, 601 South Lake, Pasadena, California 91101.

Mirin (sweet sake)   Available in Japanese markets and liquor stores as well as gourmet sections of most food markets.

Nori (thin sheets of seaweed)   Some fresh fish markets or Japanese food markets. If not stocked most markets will special order.

Parchment paper   Health food stores, gourmet and specialty shops. Larger department stores.

Sake (rice wine)   Most liquor stores and liquor departments of larger department stores.

Shallots   Most food markets stock fresh shallots. Dried or freeze-dried versions are sometimes available.

Shirataki   May be found fresh in Japanese markets or canned in gourmet and specialty foods sections of many stores.

Shitake (dried, large, black mushrooms)   Japanese food markets, gourmet sections of specialty markets.

Soybean paste   Health food stores and Japanese and specialty food markets.

Soy sauce   Most food markets; Tamari (soy) sauce at health food stores.

Squid   Many meat and fish departments of food markets, fresh fish markets and Japanese markets.

Steamer (Japanese)   This item is increasingly difficult to find even in light of the increased interest in Japanese cookery. Local inquiry will usually produce a source, but since these are usually imported from Japan, sources change. Many mail-order gift catalogues will carry these.

Swedish pancake pan   Many gourmet shops and large department stores carry these. If not available, order directly from NK Department Store, Stockholm, Sweden (allow about 6-8 weeks for delivery).

Tempura cooker   These cookers are normally to be found in gourmet cookware sections of large department stores and specialty markets. If there is a Japanese community in your area, inquire about a source. Gift catalogues are also a good source for purchase.

Tofu (Japanese bean curd) May be found in most Japanese markets or gourmet sections of large department stores in fresh cakes or powdered form. Many specialty shops will special order if not stocked.

Tuna, fresh Most fresh fish markets will have this; many will special order if not stocked.

Vegetable cubes Found in most food markets. If difficult to find, order directly from The Pantry, Marshall Fields, Mayfair, 100 and North Aves., Wauwatosa, Wisconsin 53213.

Vegetable steamer If it is impossible to find one of these in your health food store or gourmet shop, it can be ordered from Ekco-Flint Cookware Steamer, Ekco Housewares Co., 9234 West Belmont, Franklin Park, Illinois 60131.

Wire whisk Found in large food markets, hardware and specialty shops or gourmet utensil sections of department stores.

Wooden board (for *Smorgasbord*) Large bread boards from hardware and department stores are a good substitute. Order authentic ones directly from NK Department store, Stockholm, Sweden. (State size desired or approx.)

A word about specialty flours Occasionally good, whole-grained and specialty flours of quality are difficult to find, but health food stores stock most kinds. The best source for information on these flours is Director of Consumer Affairs, El Molino Mills, 345 N. Baldwin Park Blvd., City of Industry, California 91746.

Approximate Conversions from Metric Measures

Symbol	When You Know	Multiply by	To Find	Symbol
MASS (weight)				
g	grams	0.035	ounces	oz
kg	kilograms	2.2	pounds	lb
VOLUME				
ml	milliliter	0.03	fluid ounces	fl oz
l	liters	2.1	pints	pt
l	liters	1.06	quarts	qt
l	liters	0.26	gallons	gal
TEMPERATURE (exact)				
°C	Celsius temperature	9/5 then add 32	Fahrenheit temperature	°F

Index

A

B